BARRON'S BOOK NOTES

HERMANN HESSE'S

Steppenwolf & Siddhartha

BY

Ruth Goode

SERIES COORDINATOR

Murray Bromberg
Principal, Wang High School of Queens
Holliswood, New York

Past President
High School Principals Association of New York City

BARRON'S EDUCATIONAL SERIES, INC.
Woodbury, New York • London • Toronto • Sydney

ACKNOWLEDGMENTS

Our thanks to Milton Katz and Julius Liebb for their advisory assistance on the *Book Notes* series.

© Copyright 1985 by Barron's Educational Series, Inc.

All inquiries should be addressed to:
Barron's Educational Series, Inc.
113 Crossways Park Drive
Woodbury, New York 11797

Library of Congress Catalog Card No. 85-4052

International Standard Book No. 0-7641-9124-1

Library of Congress Cataloging in Publication Data
Goode, Ruth.
    Hermann Hesse's Steppenwolf & Siddhartha.

    (Barron's book notes)
    Bibliography: p. 116
    Summary: A guide to reading "Steppenwolf" and "Siddhartha" with a critical and appreciative mind encouraging analysis of plot, style, form, and structure. Also includes background on the author's life and times, sample tests, term paper suggestions, and a reading list.
    1. Hesse, Hermann, 1877–1962. Steppenwolf.
2. Hesse, Hermann, 1877–1962. Siddhartha. [1. Hesse, Hermann, 1877–1962. Steppenwolf. 2. Hesse, Hermann, 1877–1962. Siddhartha. 3. German literature—History and criticism] I. Title. II. Title: Hermann Hesse's Steppenwolf and Siddhartha. III. Series.
PT2617.E85S732 1985   833'.912   85-4052
ISBN 0-7641-9124-1

CONTENTS

HOW TO USE THIS BOOK

You have to know how to approach literature in order to get the most out of it. This *Barron's Book Notes* volume follows a plan based on methods used by some of the best students to read a work of literature.

Begin with the guide's section on the author's life and times. As you read, try to form a clear picture of the author's personality, circumstances, and motives for writing the work. This background usually will make it easier for you to hear the author's tone of voice, and follow where the author is heading.

Then go over the rest of the introductory material—such sections as those on the plot, characters, setting, themes, and style of the work. Underline, or write down in your notebook, particular things to watch for, such as contrasts between characters and repeated literary devices. At this point, you may want to develop a system of symbols to use in marking your text as you read. (Of course, you should only mark up a book you own, not one that belongs to another person or a school.) Perhaps you will want to use a different letter for each character's name, a different number for each major theme of the book, a different color for each important symbol or literary device. Be prepared to mark up the pages of your book as you read. Put your marks in the margins so you can find them again easily.

Now comes the moment you've been waiting for—the time to start reading the work of literature. You may want to put aside your *Barron's Book Notes* volume until you've read the work all the way through. Or you may want to alternate, reading the *Book Notes* analysis of each section as soon as you have finished reading the corresponding part of the original. Before you move on, reread crucial passages you don't fully understand. (Don't take this guide's analysis for granted—make up your own mind as to what the work means.)

Once you've finished the whole work of literature, you may want to review it right away, so you can firm up your ideas about what it means. You may want to leaf through the book concentrating on passages you marked in reference to one character or one theme. This is also a good time to reread the *Book Notes* introductory material, which pulls together insights on specific topics.

When it comes time to prepare for a test or to write a paper, you'll already have formed ideas about the work. You'll be able to go back through it, refreshing your memory as to the author's exact words and perspective, so that you can support your opinions with evidence drawn straight from the work. Patterns will emerge, and ideas will fall into place; your essay question or term paper will almost write itself. Give yourself a dry run with one of the sample tests in the guide. These tests present both multiple-choice and essay questions. An accompanying section gives answers to the multiple-choice questions as well as suggestions for writing the essays. If you have to select a term paper topic, you may choose one from the list of suggestions in this book. This guide also provides you with a reading list, to help you when you start research for a term paper, and a selection of provocative comments by critics, to spark your thinking before you write.

THE AUTHOR
AND HIS TIMES

The decade of the 1960s has gone down in United States history as the era of the Youth Rebellion. It was a time of campus sit-ins and college dropouts. Young people rejected the values of their elders and warned each other: "Don't trust anyone over thirty."

In contradiction to their own slogan, many of these same young people avidly read a little-known German author, already deceased (he died in 1962 at the age of eighty-five). What's more, they favored a novel he had written in 1927, when he was fifty. The writer was Hermann Hesse and the novel was *Steppenwolf*. Also popular with the rebels was *Siddhartha*, which Hesse wrote in 1922.

Hesse has been called a Neo-Romantic, meaning that his work echoes the ideas of the German Romantic movement of the late eighteenth and early nineteenth centuries. *Steppenwolf* has the melancholy, pessimism, and preoccupation with death and suicide characteristic of the Romantics, while *Siddhartha* is an example of the Romantics' fascination with distant times and places, Eastern religions, and fairy tales and legends.

Steppenwolf is the only one of Hesse's ten novels set in a twentieth-century city: all the others take place in past or future time and in exotic or imaginary places. Although modern in setting and content, the novel has numerous references to writers of the Romantic era; one of its "Immortals," the geniuses who hover above the earth, is Johann Wolfgang von Goethe (1749–1832), the greatest German writer of the period.

Like the Romantic writers, Hesse treats artists and intellectuals as outsiders in their society. In *Steppenwolf* he calls them the "Steppenwolves," untamed wolves who have strayed into the city from the steppes, the open plains. He called himself a Steppenwolf, and before writing the novel he wrote a series of peoms titled "Steppenwolf: a Bit of Diary in Verse" (later published under the title *Crisis*). This concept of the artist as a stranger in his world stems in part from the fact that Germany in the Romantic era (and until 1871) was not a unified nation but a loose collection of mostly small states. Its writers generally considered themselves citizens not of their little communities but of the world. They were scornful of the restraints of propriety and sought the freedom to experience the heights and depths of the emotions. In the same vein, *Steppenwolf*'s hero, Harry Haller, on his first appearance in the novel, is in a characteristically Romantic state of disgust with his placid day, which had held neither joy nor pain.

Hermann Hesse won the Nobel Prize for Literature in 1946, but by the late 1950s he had only a small literary following in the United States. What drew the young rebels of the 1960s to his works?

The truth is that these two novels, although written forty years earlier, addressed many of the rebellious youths' concerns and interests. *Steppenwolf*'s hero attacks commercialism, war-making, and society's indifference to the arts, and he takes a hallucinatory, possibly drug-induced "trip." *Siddhartha*, the story of a Hindu prince's exploration of the religions of his time, met the young people's interest in Eastern culture as something perhaps more relevant than what the Western world offered them.

The Eastern influence was part of Hesse's childhood as the son and grandson of missionaries who had served in India. Later, during his psychoanalysis, he would return to this atmosphere of his childhood to make a serious study of the Indian religions and their scriptures, the Vedas and Upanishads of Hinduism and the teachings of the Buddha.

Hinduism came into India with a Sanskrit-speaking nomadic people, the Aryans, about 1500 B.C., and developed into the rigid, ritualistic Brahminism against which Siddhartha rebels in the novel. A countermovement to Brahminism was Buddhism, in the fifth century B.C., which taught that each individual could achieve release from suffering without the Brahministic rituals, by following the Buddha's teaching and giving up all worldly ties. Hesse described Buddhism as the Protestant movement of Indian religion. He first embraced and then rejected the Buddhist principle as a denial of life. Siddhartha also rejects the Buddha's teaching, as he rejects all teaching, in order to find his own way to the peace of understanding.

In his native Germany, Hermann Hesse was not considered a writer of protest. He was regarded as part of the mainstream of German literature. However, his political outspokenness—as a pacifist in World War I and an anti-Nazi through the 1930s and World War II—forced him to leave Germany and to become a Swiss citizen.

In the years after World War II, Hesse was again

a popular author in Germany and received many letters from disillusioned young Germans. He also gained a vast audience in postwar Japan. In 1946 he received the Nobel Prize for Literature.

The tidal wave of American interest in Hesse came too late for him to appreciate. He envisioned America as a technological hell with no soul, and he predicted that not more than ten people in the United States would ever appreciate his work. If he had lived a few years longer he would have seen his prediction overturned. The rebels of the 1960s in the United States saw him as an advocate of the antimaterialistic counterculture, the drug culture, and the search for truth in the mystic religions of the East. Throughout the 1960s and early '70s, Hesse was one of their heroes. Vast numbers of *Steppenwolf* and *Siddhartha* were sold, and Hesse's other works were popular as well.

If his youthful followers had read Hesse's biography as avidly as they read his fiction, they would have learned that his life was as relevant to them as his novels. He was a top student, but also a rebel who ran away from one school and was expelled from another. His parents had even once engaged a faith healer to drive out the demon they believed had possessed the boy. And another time he attempted suicide.

Hesse spent his life looking within himself for the meaning of human existence. Each of his novels was in some way autobiographical, and he himself acknowledged that in all his heroes he saw "pieces of himself." *Steppenwolf* is his most openly autobiographical novel, and even *Siddhartha*, although exotic in story and setting, is a modestly disguised autobiography.

A Lifetime of Quest Herman Hesse's life was a succession of crises—like Harry Haller's life in *Steppenwolf*—and self-searching quests like both Haller's and Siddhartha's. He was born on July 2, 1877, in the little town of Calw in southwestern Germany, bordering on Switzerland. He was the second of his parents' six children. His father had served as a missionary in India and his mother had been born there. Her father had also been a missionary as well as a celebrated scholar of Indian lore and languages.

From an early age, young Hermann haunted his grandfather's library of Asian literature. His parents' house was a stopping place for missionaries and scholars returning from the East, and it was filled with Indian literature and art. Contrasting with this exposure to exotic religions was his parents' form of Christianity. As members of the Pietist sect of the Lutheran Church, they believed in a literal interpretation of the Bible. They disapproved of dancing, theater, sports, and public performances.

Hermann began composing poetry at the age of five and decided to become a writer at thirteen. At fourteen his parents enrolled him in a theological seminary, expecting him to follow family tradition and become a minister. In rebellion against the rigid school atmosphere, he ran away. His parents then entered him in a conventional school, but he was soon expelled. He was apprenticed to booksellers, worked in a clock factory, and for a time helped in his father's religious publishing company. From the age of twenty-one he worked in bookshops in the German university town of Tübingen and then in Basel, Switzerland.

Throughout these stormy years, Hesse pursued his self-education in German literature and wrote poetry and autobiographical fiction. In 1904 his first novel, *Peter Camenzind*, was published. It is the story of a young man who breaks away from his middle-class background to live close to nature. When this book met with success, he quit his job to write full-time.

That same year he married and went to live at Gaienhofen, on the German shore of Lake Constance (Bodensee). Two more novels followed (*Beneath the Wheel*, 1906, and *Gertrud*, 1910), as well as articles and reviews in German cultural journals, one of which he cofounded. A spiritual pilgrimage he took to India in 1911 proved disappointing—the ancient Eastern land he sought was already too Westernized—although the experience later bore fruit in *Siddhartha*.

The outbreak of World War I in 1914 found Hesse living in Bern, Switzerland, the country which from then on was to be his permanent home. While working on behalf of German prisoners of war, he wrote articles condemning the war and the nationalism that had led to it, becoming the target of hundreds of hate letters from Germany.

The novel *Rosshalde* in 1914, the story of an artist struggling in an unhappy marriage, reflected trouble in Hesse's own marriage. In 1916 his father died, his youngest son became seriously ill with meningitis, and his wife was committed to a mental hospital. Shaken by these blows, Hesse came close to a breakdown. He had long been interested in the work of Sigmund Freud, the founder of psychoanalysis, and of Freud's Swiss disciple, Carl Gustav Jung (1875–1961). Feeling his mental health threatened, he entered a sanitarium and underwent psychoanalysis.

The first product of this experience, the novel *Demian: the Story of a Youth*, appeared in 1919 under a pen name. It enjoyed great success and won a prize for first novels, which Hesse returned, revealing his identity. Years of productivity followed, despite periods of severe depression in the 1920s (which nevertheless yielded the novels *Siddhartha* and *Steppenwolf*).

Steppenwolf has been called a psychoanalytic novel, and some biographers describe it as a fictionalized version of Hesse's own psychoanalysis. Hesse had been interested in the system originated by Freud of bringing into the conscious mind those experiences, real and imagined, that are buried in the unconscious. The theory is that these memories have been suppressed because they are too painful to be faced, but if they are brought to light and examined they can cease to be emotionally harmful.

Freud's Swiss disciple Jung formulated his own theoretical structure of the mind, or psyche. To Freud's two psychological levels, the conscious and the unconscious, Jung added a third: the collective unconscious, a repository of the myths and symbols drawn from the shared experiences of the human race. One of Jung's archetypes, as he called these mythical images, is the Wise Old Man, who may be identified in *Siddhartha* as the old ferryman Vasudeva.

Hesse held that psychoanalysis merely confirmed what, as an artist, he already knew about the unconscious. Supporting him in this view was Freud's interpretation of the artist's role, which is to descend into the unconscious and bring back its truths in the bearable form of art. Scholars have identified many Jungian ideas in *Steppenwolf*, but Hesse felt that by the time he came to write the novel he was free of psychoanalytic guidance and could function independently as an artist.

On its appearance in 1927, Hesse's fellow author Thomas Mann wrote him that *Steppenwolf* was an experimental novel in a class with James Joyce's *Ulysses* and André Gide's *The Counterfeiters*, two highly innovative works that had been published earlier in the same decade. The experimental aspect of *Steppenwolf* has been described by some readers as its structure, which gives three different versions of the novel's hero by three imaginary authors. Others have found the novel experimental in its blend of outer and inner reality, dramatic interior monologues (passages in which the hero is thinking aloud for the reader), and a hallucinatory journey into the unconscious which to some readers is a drug-induced "trip." *Siddhartha*, by contrast, is a relatively straightforward narrative told in the form of a legend, and it has been called Hesse's most perfect novel.

Another distinction between the two novels is that while *Siddhartha* ends with its hero having attained his goal, *Steppenwolf* ends inconclusively: Harry Haller acknowledges that he must try again, and as often as necessary, to explore his inner self. This ending may be partly due to the fact that Hesse had been blocked for eighteen months in carrying the Siddhartha story to its victorious conclusion. Five years later, in *Steppenwolf*, he did not try to resolve his story but took his hero only as far as he himself had gone in learning to live with himself. He called *Steppenwolf* his catharsis, a Greek word meaning an esthetic experience that cleanses and purges the emotions, or, in psychoanalysis, a release of emotions that alleviates symptoms. The novel did this for its hero as well as for its author.

Steppenwolf

THE NOVEL

The Plot

Steppenwolf opens with a preface by a young businessman, who introduces a sheaf of notes left behind by a lodger in his attic rooms several years before. This young man, the landlady's nephew, describes the eccentric lodger, Harry Haller, who called himself a Steppenwolf, meaning in German a wolf of the steppes, or plains. The narrator finds this an odd but apt description of the shy, lonely wanderer who revealed little about himself but left a haunting memory.

The preface recounts Harry's arrival and the narrator's several encounters with him—on the stairs, at a concert and an art lecture, and in a tavern. He has decided to publish Harry Haller's "records" although he can't say whether the experiences it relates were real or fictitious.

Haller's "records," subtitled "For Madmen Only," begin with a walk in the dusk after a boring day. The walk takes Harry into an imaginary world by way of a flickering sign, an appearing and disappearing little door in a church wall, and a peddler with a placard advertising, "Magic Theater—En-

trance Not For Everybody." The peddler hands
Harry a pamphlet and vanishes. In his room again,
Harry examines the pamphlet.

It is called "Treatise on the Steppenwolf" and is
a second portrait of Harry, a psychological one this
time. It analyzes Harry as inwardly half man and
half wolf, two selves in constant conflict. It describes Harry's struggle to be himself, which has
resulted only in greater loneliness. It explains to
Harry the role of the Steppenwolves—the artists
and intellectuals—in middle-class society, and the
geniuses who break free and become Immortals.
It tells Harry that his wolf is an oversimplification,
that he has not two but hundreds of selves. Some
day he may see himself in one of the Immortals'
magic mirrors, or find in one of their magic theaters what he needs to free his soul. Finally the
anonymous authors bid Harry good-bye and cheer
him on his path toward becoming an Immortal.

Harry, again in the first person, compares what
the Treatise says of him with a poem he has written about the wolf. He finds them both true and
unbearable. He recalls the successive crises in his
life, the despair, and the new self-knowledge he
has gained each time at the cost of increased loneliness. He will not go through this again. He will
end it, commit suicide. But first, the Magic Theater.

After nights of search he finds the peddler, who
directs him to a seedy tavern. Here he meets the
bar girl Hermine, who introduces him to the prostitute Maria and the jazz musician Pablo. With
Hermine as guide, Harry learns to dance and to
enjoy sex and the night life of the city. He joins
the revelers at a masked ball.

Pablo, as master of ceremonies, invites Harry

into the Magic Theater. Here, in a series of dream-like adventures, Harry fights a war against automobiles, makes love to all the women he has ever loved, commits an imaginary murder, and prepares to be executed. Instead, he is condemned to go on living. Pablo rebukes him for messing up his magic with reality. Harry acknowledges that he will go on trying to face his inner self, and perhaps learn to do better next time.

The Characters

Harry Haller

From his initials, his age and appearance, and such references to his personal history as his wife's insanity and the newspaper abuse of him as a pacifist, Harry Haller is considered a portrait of Hermann Hesse, who was struggling out of the same depression as Haller when he wrote the novel. Harry is an intellectual, a poet, and a music lover. He does not work for a living but lives well on an income. He is desperately lonely, without home or family, living a cheerless life in a lodging house. He is full of contradictions. He despises the middle class, is disgusted by a comfortable day without pain or joy in typical middle-class moderation. Yet he chooses to live in a middle-class house and loves its cleanliness and order. He is a sensitive, civilized man but believes that under the surface is a wild wolf of the plains, and that these contradictory selves are continually at war. His adventures in the novel take him into the night world of pleasure, and then through dreamlike experiences in the Magic Theater, where he confronts not only his wolf self but many other selves that make up his personality.

In Harry's first-person narrative he is seen to be changed by these experiences, although reluctantly. At the end you are left to wonder whether he will indeed go on to make a happier life for himself. Do you think Harry is unique, or do other human beings have similar multiple personalities? Can you find examples of this in yourself, your family members, your friends? Does Harry offer a guide for confronting these many selves to make a richer and happier life?

The Nephew

The narrator of the preface is the landlady's nephew, who lives next door to Harry. He is a well-meaning young businessman of conventional habits and typical middle-class tastes, including concerts and art lectures. He is suspicious of the new lodger—who keeps irregular hours and doesn't work for living—and he is made uneasy by Harry's profound sadness. At the same time he is impressed by Harry's obvious financial respectability, and finds himself sympathetic to the eccentric lodger. Years after Harry has left, he is haunted by impressions of Harry that remain with him. Oddly, he was entirely unaware of Harry's excursion into the city's night life until he read Harry's "records." He thinks these adventures may all be fictitious, but decides to publish them anyway. The nephew gives you your only portrait of Harry as seen from outside himself.

The Landlady

The aunt, Harry's landlady, is a middle-class housewife who keeps her house in shining order.

She is a motherly woman who listens sympathetically but doesn't ask questions.

Hermine

The complete opposite of middle-class respectability, this beautiful woman is a prostitute who practices both heterosexual and homosexual love. In a motherly way she takes Harry in hand, looks after his comfort, and teaches him to enjoy pleasure. In this respect she is recognizable as a real person, but one with an aura of mystery. From one moment to the next Harry sees her as a boy, the friend of his adolescence. She understands Harry as though she has known him for years, gives him orders—which he unquestioningly obeys—and warns him that her last command will be to kill her. At this point she reveals touches of herself as unreal and magical, as part of Harry's inner state. In Hermine you see a first example of Hesse's use of names as symbols: Hermine is the feminine equivalent of Herman, the name of Harry's boyhood friend. You also see in Hermine a literary version of an image in psychoanalytic theory. She is Harry's female side, projected by him onto a real woman.

Maria

Hermine introduces Maria, a lovely young prostitute, to Harry as part of his education in pleasure. She is a total innocent who lives for the moment and suffers no guilt. Unlike Hermine, she comes across as an entirely real young woman who serves as Harry's sexual outlet.

Pablo

Pablo is both a real and a dream figure who changes with Harry's experiences. His reality is as a jazz musician and a dandy, but he also appears to be a young god of love, then a magician who takes on the guise of Mozart, Harry's supreme idol among the Immortals. As a real person Pablo dispenses drugs and leads the Masked Ball, and as a figure of magic from Harry's inner world he opens the way for Harry into the Magic Theater. Hesse concentrates in this character the jazz, sex, drugs, drinking, and dancing of the postwar youth of the 1920s (and again of the 1960s).

The Professor

Harry meets this old schoolmate on his night of exploration, but the professor turns out to be an example of the rigid, intolerant bourgeoisie which Harry detests.

Other Elements

SETTING

Harry tells his landlady that he is visiting the city to take advantage of its libraries and antiquities. The city is both old and modern, with ancient buildings and alleys in the Old Town where Harry does most of his wandering. Hesse's biographers identify it as drawn from both Basel and Zurich, two Swiss cities in which he lived at different times.

The house where Harry takes lodgings is middle-class and immaculately kept. Harry's sitting room is a place of artistic disorder, littered with papers, cigar ash, wine bottles, and well-worn

books. A Buddha from Siam (Thailand), a portrait
of the Indian pacifist leader Mahatma Gandhi, and
watercolors by Harry himself are among its deco-
rations. In the evening he frequents an old-fashioned tavern where lonely men like himself sit,
each at his own little table, sipping wine and
speaking to no one.

Walking in the Old Town on a wet night, Harry
sees a door in an ancient wall that was not there
before, a flickering sign advertising MAGIC
THEATER—ENTRANCE NOT FOR EVERYBODY and colored letters reflected on the wet asphalt reading
FOR MADMEN ONLY! A peddler directs him to a bar
and dance hall, where he meets Hermine. On his
rounds of pleasure with Hermine he goes to dances,
night clubs, and cafes. The final setting is the hall
of the Masked Ball, patterned after the Zurich artists' annual costume ball, which Hesse attended
with a party of friends. This changes to the Magic
Theater, a place both real and unreal, that resembles the mezzanine floor of a theater, with doors
opening into boxes that face the stage. But here,
each of the boxes has its own imaginary spectacle
at which Harry is both audience and participant.

Interwoven with these external settings, especially the realistic scenes, are the internal settings
of Harry's monologues, the streams of memory,
emotion, and ideas in which he shares his conscious mind with the reader. The opening pages
of his "records" describe such an external-internal
state-of-mind setting: the contrast between his
tranquil day and his detestation of middle-class
tranquility. Another state-of-mind setting occurs
as he sits over his meal in the old-fashioned tavern, and a remembered piece of music stirs him to

the momentary recovery of an exalted state he calls his "golden track." As you read, watch for other inner settings along Harry's route.

Under Hesse's skillful hand the dividing line between the reality of the Old Town and Harry's fantasy of it is never clear. Can you, reading carefully, spot the devices by which Hesse achieves his effect?

THEMES

The following are major themes of *Steppenwolf*.

1. THE OUTSIDER

Harry Haller's name for himself, the steppenwolf, stamps him as an outsider. A wolf of the plains can never be part of human society. The nephew agrees that this is an apt designation of the shy, homeless, and homesick creature that lurks behind Harry's sensitive and civilized exterior. Harry himself analyzes his separateness. He is unable to share the aims or pleasures of people who crowd into the hotels and cafes with the oppressive jazz music and entertainments that many people enjoy. Beyond these forms of mass pleasure, he also deplores the conventions, the commercialism, and the complacency of the middle-class world. He is forever an alien in this world. His moments of joy come spontaneously, from a line of poetry or a passage of remembered music, as moments of expanded spirit that he calls the "golden track." This concept of the artist and intellectual as an alien among ordinary people is an echo of the Romantic era in German literature when artists held themselves to be citizens of the world, free of the conventions of their individual societies. But at the beginning of the novel, Harry doesn't think of this as freedom, but as alienation and loneliness. Thus the stage is set for Harry's entrance into the world of pleasure. Does Harry benefit from this experience?

2. PREOCCUPATION WITH DEATH

Suicide, murder, and execution track their way through the novel, but it is all quite bloodless. The nephew in the Preface and the anonymous authors of the Treatise describe Harry's deprived and cheerless way of life as suicidal, and the Treatise gives him permission to take his life when he turns fifty in two years. Harry will not wait, however. He will put an end to his misery now though not exactly at this moment. He finds comfort in the idea that he can always end it if life becomes truly unbearable: the door of escape is open. The preoccupation with death is presented in other forms: the wholesale murder of the automobile hunt, the murder of Hermine, and finally, as Harry is judged and prepares to be executed. But the automobile hunt is one of the Magic Theater fantasies, the murder of Hermine is the reflection of a girl stabbed with the reflection of a knife, and Harry is condemned to live, not to die. In actuality Harry would be incapable of any such acts of violence. Yet each of these scenes releases violent emotions, as though the events were real, but without the dire consequences of reality.

3. MULTIPLE SELVES

The Treatise portion of *Steppenwolf* tells Harry that he is mistaken in believing that the civilized man and the wolf are his only two selves. Each human being is composed of hundreds, perhaps thousands of selves. By limiting his personality to only two, Harry has cut himself off from a veritable Garden of Eden of selves. He will not find inner peace until he confronts and acknowledges all these other aspects of his personality, and realizes that they are not necessarily in conflict. In the search for his other selves, Harry plunges into the world of pleasure and then into his inner world as revealed to him in the Magic Theater. What other selves does Harry discover in the course of his adventures? What other selves are you aware of in your own personality? Do you think of them as compatible or at war with each other?

4. JUNGIAN IDEAS

Hermann Hesse said after his psychoanalysis with a pupil of Carl Gustav Jung that it had confirmed his artist's intuition of what lies hidden in the unconscious. In *Steppenwolf* he used none of the terms of Jungian theory—since he was writing a novel and not a textbook—but he did make use of Jungian ideas.

Harry Haller's wolf self can be seen as the "shadow" in Jungian theory, the side of Harry's personality unacceptable to his conscious self.

Hermine represents the female element that exists in every male. The Jungian term for this is "anima," and it is suppressed as the unacceptable feminine weakness of the outwardly strong male. To protect his image, the man does not recognize his anima as part of himself but projects the anima on a woman in his life. He sees his wife or lover not as herself but as his own unconscious female counterpart. You can see this in the dialogue between Harry and Hermine, when they both acknowledge how much she resembles Harry in thoughts and feelings. Notice how readily—and comfortably—he accepts her rebukes and follows her advice.

Magic, as in Pablo's Magic Theater, is a Jungian synonym for the unconscious. And Harry does indeed act out his unconscious, suppressed violence in the automobile hunt, the taming of the wolf and then the man, and the murder of Hermine. Harry's longing for suicide, in Jung's and Harry's interpretations, is a way to avoid facing one's unconscious. There are other bits of psychological wisdom in the novel: opposites are two sides of the same thing, self-hate is sheer egotism, and you cannot love your neighbor unless you love yourself. Do you agree with any of these? Disagree?

5. THE DECLINE OF CIVILIZATION

Harry Haller sees Western civilization in decline. He refers to the loss of cultural values and the preparations already being made (in the 1920s) for yet another war. He offers a theory that civilization is in transition between one era and the next, and he proposes that some individuals suffer extremely during these transitions. The nephew in his Preface suggests that Haller is such a sufferer—that Haller's sickness of the soul is a sickness of the time. Whether this post-World War I period was only a time of great change but not of civilization's decline is debatable. Some would say that World War II proves Harry was right. Do you think Haller's despair for civilization is justified in light of later events?

STYLE

When Hesse's novel was published in 1927, it was considered experimental for its time in several ways. One innovation was that he wrote in three different styles, each conforming to a different narrator. Each of them gives its own version of Harry Haller and his five-week fantasy adventure. (William Faulkner used similar techniques in such works as *The Sound and the Fury*, 1929, and *As I Lay Dying*, 1930.)

The Preface, by the nephew of Haller's landlady, is a sober account by a young middle-class businessman of the aunt's eccentric lodger. It is an objective description of Haller as seen from the outside, and the writing style is uninspired. It is the conscientious effort of an educated person who is not a writer.

Next, introduced by Harry himself, is the Treatise on the Steppenwolf. It is presented as a pamphlet handed to Harry by a street peddler. The author is unidentified, but he offers sly hints that he is one of Harry's Immortals, the ghosts of great men like the composer Mozart and the writer Goethe who hover in the ether above earth and whose laughter Harry hears now and then. Just as the Preface portrayed Harry's outer person, the Treatise describes his inner self. The style is that of a teacher: critical, rather patronizing, and with an occasional jab of humor at Harry's expense. The tone is often preachy, and sometimes the meaning seems deliberately obscure.

Harry has already introduced himself in the first person, recounting how he came to possess the Treatise. In Harry's own narrative you come at last

to the evocative, flexible, and varied style of a writer.
For example, he begins by describing the "lukewarm" day he has just spent and the sequence of
long, slow-moving sentences matches the slow
passing of hours with neither joy nor pain. After
giving you the text of the Treatise, he continues
with a blend of description, dialogue, and interior
monologues—passages in which he recalls his past,
reveals his loves and hates, and examines his state
of mind.

His first crossing from the real to the unreal comes
with the sight of a flickering electric sign on an
ancient wall, and the barely discernible letters reflected in the wet pavement. The imagery of reflections and mirrors recurs again and again: in the
Treatise, in a teasing reference to "our" magic mirrors, and in the Magic Theater. There Harry's mirrored self is symbolically shattered into his multiple selves. He and the wolf are mirrored both
separately and together. Finally, Hermine is a reflection of a girl murdered by a reflection of a knife.
In passages of reality, such as the dinner in the
professor's house and the first meeting with Hermine in the Black Eagle Bar, the style is brisk and
the dialogue lively and natural. But even as the
characters and events undergo dreamlike transformations, Harry tells it as though it is all really happening—in a narrative voice and with intense
emotions but no surprise, however grotesque the
events.

The translation by Basil Creighton, dating from
1929, was the first and is still the only one in English.
Originally for an English audience, it contains such
British usages as "gramophone" for phonograph
and "post" for mail. A revised version by Joseph

Mileck and Horst Frenz, Americanizing and up-
dating the Creighton translation, appears in Holt,
Rinehart and Winston hardcover editions from 1963
on, and in the Bantam paperback editions from
1969.

POINT OF VIEW

Since *Steppenwolf* is composed of three different
first-person narratives, each of them contributes to
the story of Harry Haller from a different point of
view. The narrator of the Preface, the landlady's
nephew, is a man of conventional opinions and
prejudices who gives a portrait of Haller as he appears to the middle-class world. However, he makes
some shrewd observations about Harry Haller's
gifts, his unhappiness, and his way of life, which
this observer calls "suicidal."

The second point of view is that of the Treatise
on the Steppenwolf. The pamphlet is a psychological portrait of Harry. It is written in the first-person plural, but this appears to be an editorial "we"
until near the end of the Treatise, when it refers
to "our" mirrors and "our" Magic Theaters. From
this hint the authors appear to be the ghostly Immortals whom Harry admires and hopes to join.

As the authors of the Treatise, the Immortals are
all-knowing—indeed, they know more about Harry
than anyone other than Harry himself. They explain the confusions and contradictions in his personality. They know his past and present life and
they predict his possible future. They pass judgment on Harry's errors in self-understanding and
instruct him how to do better. Their tone is that of

patient professors speaking to a student who tries hard but is not very bright.

The third narrator is Harry Haller himself, and the novel becomes his first-person account of a magical, dreamlike experience. This narrative, which forms the bulk of the novel, has been interpreted in several ways: as a hallucinatory, drug-induced "trip," as a record of the author's actual psychoanalysis, and as an artist's exploration of his own dream world.

The first interpretation—that the novel represents a drug-induced "trip"—triggered the wave of popularity for both the book and its author with the American drug culture of the Sixties. Ironically, this is the least likely of the three interpretations. Hesse's biographers are all in agreement that this respectable middle-aged intellectual was neither a drug user nor an advocate of drug use. His most radical, "anti-establishment" principles were his anti-war and anti-Nazi stands.

One possibility for you to consider is that all three points of view are intended by the author as Harry Haller's—or Hesse's—own view of himself. The first narrator is Haller/Hesse imagining how he appears to the middle-class society that he detests. The second, the "we" of the Treatise, would be a psychological self-portrait as he might see himself, looking down like the Immortals from a detached, superior height. The third is Haller/Hesse pursuing the solution to his difficulties through the labyrinth of his unconscious.

Obviously Hesse, as the author, is the creator of all three narrators. But if you like this further twist—that both the nephew's and the Immortals' account of Haller are also Haller's own creations—then you may see in it a streak of Hesse's humor.

FORM AND STRUCTURE

Steppenwolf is a "framework" novel, meaning that it has a realistic introduction to a narrative that may be unrealistic. The framework form provides a contrast between the commonsense Preface and the dreamlike adventures that constitute the body of the novel. The Preface gives an objective portrait of Harry Haller. Although it appears as an introduction, the Preface is presented as having been written some years after Haller has gone, and it covers the whole period of his stay in the lodging house.

A second departure from conventional narrative is the "Treatise on the Steppenwolf," the mysterious pamphlet that gives Harry a psychological portrait of himself at the beginning of his adventure. In most editions this section is physically set off from the body of the novel by a change in type and page layout, as though it were in fact a pamphlet bound into the volume.

The main body of the novel is called "Harry Haller's Records," with the subheading "For Madmen Only." The first-person narrative that begins here flows steadily forward, with no chapter divisions but only occasional spaces in the text to indicate a change of time or scene. The crossings between the real and the imaginary are not signaled except by content.

The story appears to follow chronological order but, like the characters and events, time also has a dreamlike distortion, being sometimes stretched, sometimes compressed. Harry refers confusingly to things happening "today," "yesterday," "last night." Only by reading carefully can you determine that Harry's entire adventure, excluding the Preface but including his acquiring and reading the Treatise, takes place within a period of five or six weeks.

Breaking into the narrative flow of Harry's adventures are his interior monologues, in which he bares his thoughts and memories to the reader. These offer still another portrait of Harry, an intellectual one, revealing his observations and opinions on the world around him, its arts, and the state of its society. They also serve as flashbacks, giving his personal history before the time of the novel.

The Magic Theater experience carries the novel to its climax. Here Harry experiences past, future, and present as they exist together in his unconscious where memories, hopes, and unfulfilled drives are forever stored. His adventures sweep tumultuously to his predicted murder of Hermine, and then decline from that high point to end without a clear resolution of Harry's fate, except that he will go on living and trying.

In terms of literary experiment, the framework form is not new. But the blend of outer and inner worlds, political and social argument, and experiences drawn from the unconscious—all in terms of the hero's quest for self-realization—constitute a literary innovation for its time. When you read *Steppenwolf*, you will actually read three books with three authors, three points of view, and three portraits of Harry. Some see the Magic Theater sequence as a fourth portrait. Do you?

The Story

Steppenwolf is not divided into chapters. Rather, there are headings only for a preface and three major narrative segments. The "Preface" is the introduction by the landlady's nephew. "Harry Haller's Records," with the subheading " 'For Madmen Only,' " begins the first-person narrative by the novel's central figure. "Treatise on the Steppenwolf" breaks in on this narrative within a few pages. The story then continues in Harry's first person without further divisions. To help your understanding of Harry's story, chapter subdivisions have been added.

PREFACE

Steppenwolf uses three different first-person narrators; this is the first. Its supposed author offers it rather apologetically to introduce the "records" left behind by Harry Haller some years before, which this narrator plans to publish. The Preface was therefore written several years after the events recounted, and covers the whole period of the novel itself.

As the nephew of the lodging house landlady, this narrator occupied the rooms next door to Haller's and thus had numerous encounters with the man. In describing Haller, he reveals himself as a well-meaning but stodgy young businessman of conventional habits and tastes. He disapproves of Haller's irregular hours and obvious lack of employment, but in the end he responds sympathetically to the eccentric stranger. Some years have passed since Haller left, but the narrator confesses that he is still haunted by the disturbing, yet somehow appealing impression Haller made on him.

NOTE: The Preface is used to give a realistic introduction to memoirs that may or may not be real. Hesse also used this "framework" device for two other novels. Can you offer one strength and one weakness of this technique?

Steppenwolf has been called the most autobiographical of Hesse's novels, and the narrator's first paragraphs bear this out. His description of Haller is identical with that of Hesse at the time he was writing the novel. To paint his self-portrait through the eyes of a member of the middle-class that he so despised may strike you as Hesse's private joke. At the same time, it has a serious literary purpose. It sets before you in ordinary terms the character in whose company you are to make a fantastic journey. The more believable the Preface makes Harry Haller, the more convincing will be his adventures.

The nephew says he was at first uneasy with this lodger's foreign air, his eccentric ways, and his request that the landlady spare him the formality of notifying the police of his residence, as required in European countries. To this day the

nephew knows nothing of where the man came
from or what his business or profession may have
been. Haller explained only that he came to make
use of the city's libraries and to enjoy its antiquities.

Haller's intellectual face, his polite and friendly
manner, and a sadness about him slowly changed
the unfavorable impression he made at first. Yet
the man's description of himself as a wolf of the
steppes seemed appropriate. He was just the kind
of creature that a wolf might be if he had strayed
into town.

Haller arrived with a big case of books and two
trunks, one plastered with travel labels from abroad,
the other of very fine leather which impressed this
bourgeois young man. Obviously the new lodger
was not poor.

The nephew goes on compulsively with his description—Haller's look of an uncommonly gifted
man, the mobile play of expression, the thoughtful
conversation. He calls Haller a genius of suffering.
In a burst of insight he surmises that Haller was
brought up by strict, pious parents who failed to
break the boy's independent spirit and only taught
him to hate himself. Yet Haller strove earnestly to
love others. Here the narrator, with surprising per-
ceptiveness, observes that to love one's neighbor
one must love oneself, and that self-hate is really
the same thing as self-centeredness.

These nuggets of psychological wisdom seem out
of character in a young man so materialistic. Is
Hesse giving this character insights that such a man
could not have? The young man does aspire to
artistic and intellectual interests, it seems. He sees

Haller at a concert. He invites Haller to an art lecture. How would you explain the apparent contradictions in this character?

A significant encounter occurs when the nephew
finds Haller sitting on the stairs, admiring the aunt's
immaculate little vestibule (foyer) with its potted
plants. Haller confesses that he regards the place
as a kind of temple.

NOTE: One of the plants is an araucaria, which
is a familiar middle-class houseplant. Hesse uses
the phrase "shining, well-tended, exotic araucaria" throughout as a kind of shorthand reference
to the safe middle-class life that he both loves and
abhors.

Haller's avowed admiration for the spotless
plants, the shining cleanliness, and the smells of
floor wax and furniture polish is the first reference
to a paradox. He detests everything middle-class,
yet likes to live in its tidy, orderly surroundings.
How would you explain this inconsistency in Haller's personality? Think of other situations that evoke
contradictory emotions, for example, the fascination and revulsion of a street accident.

The narrator now decides that he has told enough
about Haller's "suicidal" existence, as he calls it.
(The reference to Haller's suicidal way of life comes
up again later, in the Treatise by another, more
mysterious author.) The nephew is certain, however, that after Haller paid his bill and left—without a word of farewell—he didn't kill himself but

is going up and down the stairs in other lodging houses, pursuing his comfortless existence.

Turning to the "records" Haller left behind, the nephew finds them partly diseased, partly beautiful and thoughtful. He would have thrown them away, but his acquaintance with Haller has helped him to understand them. He has a theory that the records are more than the fancies of a disturbed mind. He believes that Haller's sickness of soul is a sickness of the times. Haller once talked of people of each era being able to live with the sufferings of their own time—the horrors of the Middle Ages, he had said, were not horrible to medieval people. But a generation can be caught in the transition between one era and the next, unable to accept the conditions of life because the conditions are changing. The nephew believes that Harry Haller is caught between two eras, and is therefore fated to live out the riddle of human destiny at a level of personal torture.

Again this young man shows himself to be more thoughtful and less rigid than you might have expected. He gives credit for the theory of transition to Haller, but he is imaginative enough to accept and enlarge on it. He now leaves you with Haller's manuscript, making no judgment on whether it is truth or fiction, suggesting instead that the reader decide for himself. The nephew's persistent uneasiness with the manuscript's contents and with his recollections of its author warns you of something unusual to come.

NOTE: Observe Hesse's skill in writing in the person of the character he has created—a flat-footed, painstaking style, just what you would expect of an educated person who was not accustomed to expressing himself in writing. Watch for the contrast with the Treatise, and with the style when Haller takes over the narrative.

HARRY HALLER'S RECORDS

"FOR MADMEN ONLY"

Harry Haller's first-person narrative is presented under these two titles. From here on, the novel is continuous—except for the inserted Treatise and occasional spaces in the text to indicate a change of scene or a lapse of time. Watch how Hesse deals with both of these—the shift from reality to fantasy and back again, and the expansion and contraction of time—two technical aspects of the novel that you may find worth following.

Harry begins by describing the day just past as a day without either joy or pain, a "lukewarm" day of contentment that he detests most. He flees from the hateful comfort of his room to the dark and foggy street. On the way downstairs he stops, illogically, to savor the middle-class orderliness of the little foyer with its potted plants, his "temple."

NOTE: The style of this passage echoes Harry's detestably comfortable day in three long, slow sentences, two paragraphs, and a total of 450 words. Watch how sentences take on a brisker rhythm as the pace of the story quickens.

Harry walks through the damp, narrow streets in the dusk. He is remembering his youth, when rain, storms, and lonely winter scenes moved him to write poetry. He still occasionally glimpses what he calls the golden track of inspired moments. He can't understand the pleasures of crowded bars and mass entertainments. He is in truth a steppenwolf, a beast of the wild, lost in the world of men.

He has often walked here, but now he sees a small doorway that he has never seen before, and then a flickering sign: MAGIC THEATER—ENTRANCE NOT FOR EVERYBODY, and then FOR MADMEN ONLY! Baffled and chilled, he takes refuge in his usual tavern, one frequented by solitary men like himself. With his vision of the little door and the flickering sign, he has made his first crossing into an imaginary dimension.

NOTE: The advertisement of the Magic Theater, NOT FOR EVERYBODY and FOR MADMEN ONLY! does more than quicken Harry's (and your) interest. It also refers to a psychological theory, popular at the time, that artistic talent was a sign of neurosis and that genius was closely related to insanity. FOR MADMEN ONLY is Hesse's allusion to that belief.

Harry eats a simple meal, drinks some pleasant wine, and is transported by a remembered bit of music into happy recollections. In a lovely bit of imagery, he compares the recollected melody to a soap bubble floating aloft, reflecting the world in miniature on its rainbow surface. He calls such moments of exalted spirit recapturing the "golden track"—would you call them consciousness-expanding?

Homeward bound, he is jolted by the raw sound of jazz from a dance hall. To Harry this is the music of decadence, miserable noise compared with "real" music such as that of Bach and Mozart. His detestation of jazz is combined with a secret hankering for it: he feels that its savage gaiety touches an "underworld of instinct" and has an honest sensuality. He prefers it to the academic music of his own day. The melody of jazz is like sugar and full of sentimentality but the rest is savage and vigorous, and the two parts go well together. He likes its sincerity, its childlike happiness. He finds it has something not only of the Black but of the American, who seems boyishly fresh and childlike to Europeans. He wonders whether he and the others who revere Europe's culture of the past are just a pigheaded minority devoted to a ghost long dead. Haller here is expressing the depression of intellectuals following World War I, when much of Europe's culture, especially Germany's, seemed to have been swept away forever. His ambivalence toward jazz, which he scorns and yet finds secretly attractive, is something to remember when you come to his later adventures.

Harry passes the old wall again—no flickering sign now, no little doorway. But a lone peddler suddenly appears, carrying a placard on which Harry reads, in dancing, reeling letters, ANARCHIST EVENING ENTERTAINMENT—MAGIC THEATER—ENTRANCE NOT FOR EVERYBODY. Harry runs after the man, asking where the entertainment is, offering to buy something from him. The man hands him a booklet and disappears through a doorway.

At home again, Harry finds in his pocket the little book, poorly printed on cheap paper like the fortunetelling pamphlets sold on street corners. With a sense of impending fate he reads its title: "Treatise on the Steppenwolf. Not for Everybody."

From its languid beginning, the story has now become filled with suspense and the promise of interesting, perhaps even sinister events. How has Hesse accomplished this? As you review the devices he uses, you will see that he has taken you across the reality-fantasy boundary not once but twice. Now you are back in Harry's room and apparently back in reality. But are you? The street peddler's booklet is directly addressed to Harry as the Steppenwolf. How can that be? Is this really a pamphlet from a peddler?

TREATISE ON THE STEPPENWOLF

NOTE: The Treatise is set apart from the rest of the novel by its style of writing and also, in most editions, by its type and page layout. In the original German edition it was printed on different paper and in the old-fashioned, elaborate German typeface called Gothic. It was further set apart by colored pages at its beginning and end, and looked like a pamphlet bound into the novel.

The Treatise begins like a fairy tale with "There was once a man, Harry," and goes on rather playfully with a discussion of Harry's idea of himself as a wolf. It points out that this is not exceptional, that many individuals live comfortably with some animal traits in their make-up. Harry's human self, however, was at war with his wolfish self. When Harry was noble and refined, the wolf snarled in scorn, judging all human activities to be absurd, stupid, and vain. But when Harry behaved as a wolf, baring his teeth and hating human beings for their lying and degenerate ways, the human Harry called him brute and spoiled his pleasure in the healthy expression of his animal nature.

So Harry was unhappy. Here the Treatise throws out some commonplace comments: that everyone feels his own unhappiness as the greatest that anyone endures, that even the unhappiest life has its sunny moments, "little flowers of happiness between sand and stone." But Harry was unhappy and made others unhappy, especially those who loved him. Most often they loved only one side of him and were disappointed when the refined and interesting man showed his fierce wolfish side, or when the wild, exciting wolf turned out to love Mozart and poetry, and to believe in human goodness. (Wolfgang Amadeus Mozart, the eighteenth-century composer and musical genius, is one of Harry's chief Immortals.) Usually those who loved the wolf were the more bitterly disappointed. Yet even Harry had his moments when both sides came together in harmony.

There are others like Harry, mostly artists, who do not have the orderly form of a career but are tossed on a perpetual tide of pain. But they have their moments of beauty when they produce works of art that give them and the world the greatest happiness. Such people sometimes feel that human life is a bad joke and a natural catastrophe, and at other times that man is a child of the gods and destined for immortality.

A Profile of Harry

The Treatise then gives a synopsis of Harry's personal history. He was a night person, with a need for solitude and independence for which he would sacrifice everything. He rejected all routine, would not work in an office or take orders from anyone. In the end he won too much of both freedom and solitude. Although he had friends, he had no real ties. He became one of the "suicides," people who might never actually take their own lives but who live like persons doomed to end that way. Although emotional and sensitive, they are often sturdy people—but at the least shock they think of suicide. In some, including Harry, the notion of suicide makes everything bearable because an emergency exit is always open. Harry had appointed his fiftieth birthday as the day on which he would take his razor and end all his pains.

Though the Steppenwolf saw himself as an outsider and looked down on ordinary men, he still lived like one. He had money in the bank, dressed correctly, and resided in respectable bourgeois houses. He never joined the criminal classes, and although he admired political criminals and revolutionaries he was never one of them.

The Middle Class

The middle class is the Treatise's next subject. The bourgeois man carefully walks a middle path, avoiding extremes of joy or pain, saintliness or viciousness. He has sacrificed intensity of experience for comfort and security. The Treatise describes the democratic forms of majority rule, the rule of law, and the vote as middle-class devices. The middle class would be overcome by its own weakness and anxiety, were it not for the Steppenwolves, the artists and intellectuals living on its fringes and providing the vitality of art and ideas.

The Immortals

Only the strongest of these outsiders can break completely out of their bourgeois heritage into the cosmos. Here you find the first reference in the Treatise to the Immortals, as Harry calls them. The Treatise describes them as living in "starry space" and going down "in splendor," but doesn't explain them. Are you to understand that these are the true geniuses, who earn immortality by their undying works of art? Harry's chief Immortals, at least those whom he names, are Mozart and Goethe.

Those who yearn to break through but never can, the Treatise continues, must find their escape through humor, which is perhaps the most brilliant achievement of the spirit. Humor makes it possible to be in the world and yet not of it, to be law-abiding and have possessions and yet be above the law and the possessions. Humor could make the Steppenwolf's suffering bearable and productive. But he must be willing to look into himself. Harry may one day get hold of one of "our" little mirrors or find what he needs in one of "our" magic theaters. Harry is aware of this need to examine himself but fears it.

Theory of Multiple Selves

Finally, says the Treatise, the Steppenwolf is a fiction. Harry is not two but a hundred or a thousand selves. Human beings regard the self as a unit by false analogy with the body, which is a single entity. Now Hesse's Indian background comes through, as he points out that in the epic poems of India the heroes are not one-dimensional individuals but entire series of incarnations, and that the Yoga technique of Buddhism is designed to break through the illusion of the personality. In a passing criticism of the Immortal, Goethe, the Treatise comments on Faust's complaint, "Two souls, alas, inhabit in my breast!"

NOTE: Faust is the scholar hero of Goethe's famous poetic drama *Faust*. Like Haller, Faust strives to understand himself and human nature. The "two souls" he refers to represent both a personal inner conflict and a conflict between literary forms. One "soul" represents Faust's passionate side and the emotional orientation of Romantic literature. The other "soul" stands for Faust's rational side, as well as the restrained ideals of ancient classical literature.

The Treatise here scolds Faust for restricting his selves to only two, just as Harry has been doing.

Harry's suffering is partly due to his effort to pack his many aspects into either his human or his wolf self. Man is not a fixed form but a transition between nature and spirit. By a bourgeois compromise, a little of both natural instinct and spiritual idealism is permitted, but any excess is condemned as either criminal or heretic.

The Steppenwolf suspects these truths but is still unwilling to make the sacrifice of himself that leads to immortality. Here the Treatise seems deliberately obscure about what it takes to achieve this. It explains Mozart not by his special musical gift but by his indifference to bourgeois ideals and his powers of suffering.

Returning to the Steppenwolf, the Treatise points out that there is no way to be wholly man or wholly wolf, and that even a wolf is not a simple creature. Wishing to be a child again is also useless, for even children are full of conflicts and complexities. Instead of narrowing one's world, one should take the whole world into one's soul, as did Buddha and every great man. The Treatise tells Harry that he has genius enough to attempt this quest for true manhood.

A man who can understand Buddha and the heaven and hell of humanity should not live in a world of common sense and democracy. Harry allows an entire Garden of Eden of opposite qualities to be locked away in the wolf, and confines the real man in him to a bourgeois existence. What he can't classify as either wolf or man he doesn't see at all.

Here the Treatise bids Harry good-bye, with the encouraging prophecy that when at last he achieves his goal among the Immortals he will look back and smile in pity at the Steppenwolf.

Thus in some twenty-five closely printed pages the Treatise draws a portrait of both Harry and the middle-class world, raising in the course of it some provocative questions: In what ways is the democratic form of government merely a middle-class device? If democracy is not suitable to the highly developed man that the Treatise admires, what form of government would be? Or would such men need any government at all?

In this description, the artist's life is full of misery except for those exalted moments when he or she produces a work of art. Is that your impression? If you have read biographies of great artists, writers, and composers, or have seen documentaries on them, do you gather that they are suffering most of the time? Or do they seem to be enjoying their work most of the time? Could that description of the misery of the artist's life be mostly a description of Hesse's own life?

Humor as a way of making life bearable is an interesting idea. To be able to laugh off your troubles indicates a certain detachment from life, as though you did not need to be involved. Do you think that is always a good thing? Can you imagine situations in which treating a problem with humor might have unfortunate consequences?

The Treatise is certainly right about children not being simple one-dimensional creatures. But when a person expresses a longing to be a child again, is he or she longing for simplicity? Isn't it rather the state of being cared for, of having grownups to look out for one—of having little or no responsibility—that one is wishing for? Isn't it the responsibilities, rather than the complexities of character, that they will face, that makes many adolescents anxious about becoming adults?

The more carefully you read the Treatise, the more you might suspect that its author is no ghostly Immortal, but none other than Harry Haller himself, who has taken this unusual way of analyzing himself. It is also a signpost pointing in the direction the story is taking, toward less realistic adventures, with magic mirrors and magic theaters to come.

NOTE: With its teaching and preaching tone of voice, sometimes scolding, sometimes sympa-

thetic and persuasive, the Treatise has been compared with the religious tracts that Hesse helped
his missionary father print in the publishing house
in Calw during the period that he spent at home
after running away from his apprenticeship in a
bookshop. Hesse seems to have been echoing his
father's theological tracts in the style of the Treatise.

Harry Haller's Records

Harry has read and reread the Treatise. He finds
a despairing verse he wrote recently about himself
as the wolf. He dismisses it as nonsense.

NOTE: Hesse was equally famous as a poet and
novelist. Germans considered him one of their finest
poets since Heinrich Heine (1797–1859). The poem
Harry finds is a poem by Hesse in the group titled
"Steppenwolf: a Bit of Diary in Verse," written while
he was planning the novel, later published (1928)
with the title *Crisis*. It is a gory hunting poem with
sexual implications.

Both the Treatise and the poem impress him as
truthful—and both fill him with despair. He falls
into one of his interior monologues, in this case a
flashback recalling past crises: his disgrace as a
pacifist and the loss of his vocation (meaning his
audience as a writer), his wife's insanity with the
resulting loss of his home and family. Each time
his life has been shattered and he has remade it,
each time with some new insight gained but at the

cost of a more solitary and sadder life than before. He sees himself as an outsider to all aspects of society, and he doubts whether all his efforts to rebuild his life in the past were worthwhile. Now he faces another such effort, but this time he will not go through with it. He will make an end of it.

NOTE: Haller's list of crises is Hesse's own: his pacifism in World War I when many Germans branded him a traitor, his wife's insanity, his permanent self-exile to Switzerland. Hesse was suffering from a severe depression when he began to write *Steppenwolf*. Haller's crisis is also a form of depression.

The choice of suicide as a way of avoiding a confrontation with the self is recognized in psychoanalytic theory, and Harry states it in these terms. He has attempted suicide before, with an overdose of the opium he takes for his gout and arthritis. This time he will do it properly, with a razor or a gun.

The Treatise teasingly suggested that he wait until he is fifty—two years more—but the door to escape stands open. Daylight is dawning when he finally goes to bed.

Waking at noon, Harry has not changed his mind about suicide but he is now preoccupied with the events of the previous evening. He sets out to find the vanishing door, the flickering sign, the peddler. He follows a funeral, accosts a man he takes to be the peddler, and is told to go to a tavern called the Black Eagle. He meets a young professor he knows and gratefully accepts an invitation while the other Harry within him grins at his hypocrisy.

The visit is a disaster. The professor talks of someone named Haller as a pacifist and traitor. The professor's wife has a sentimental portrait of Goethe that outrages Harry, who makes some rude remarks and leaves.

Hermine, Maria, Pablo

Harry walks the streets, afraid to go home. He is determined to commit suicide but is terrified of dying. Chilled and exhausted, he finds himself at the Black Eagle, the tavern and dance hall that the peddler at the funeral recommended. There Harry meets a bar girl who invites him to sit down, and a new adventure begins.

The bar girl is no ordinary prostitute. When Harry tells her about his dinner at the professor's house, she doesn't hesitate to rebuke Harry for having acted childishly. As the lively conversation continues, she exhibits an insight into Harry that seems almost clairvoyant. She takes him in charge, ordering wine and food for him and commanding him to eat and drink, teasing him because he knows Latin and Greek but never learned to dance. She coaxes him into telling her his name (but she won't tell him hers), that he is divorced but has a sweetheart although not nearby, and why he is afraid to go home. When she goes off to dance, promising to come back, she orders him to take a nap. Obediently, he falls asleep.

He dreams of being a reporter waiting for an interview with Goethe. He is bothered by a scorpion climbing up his leg, and shakes it off but doesn't dare search for it. He is confused about whether he is waiting for some other Romantic poet, but Goethe at last appears, pompous and ministerial. Haller as reporter begins his interview by accusing Goethe of insincerity. Goethe understood the hopeless struggle of human beings to achieve the eternal of the spirit and the lost innocence of nature while locked into the mortality of a lifetime. At the same time, Goethe in his long life pretended to have discovered the eternal but only mummified it, and to have spiritualized nature but only hid it with a pretty mask.

Goethe replies by referring to Mozart's opera, *The Magic Flute*, Harry's favorite. But, says Harry, Mozart did not pretend to be so important—he simply sang his divine music and died. (Mozart died at the age of 35.) Goethe amiably apologizes for having lived to be eighty-two. He admits that he feared death, longed to live to one hundred, and that to the end of his life he had a child's curiosity and love of play.

At that the old man straightens and becomes rosy and youthful, and the star of some honorary order on his breast blossoms into wildflowers. He whispers into Harry's ear that Harry must not take old dead people so seriously: "We immortals like joking," he says. Seriousness is an accident of time, and in eternity there is no time. Eternity is a mere moment, just long enough for a joke, says the old man, and he breaks into a merry dance. So Goethe learned to dance, Harry thinks in his dream.

Harry asks about Molly, a heroine of the Romantic era, and Goethe offers him a tiny effigy of a woman's leg, which turns into the scorpion. With this he teases Harry, meanwhile changing back into an old man, a thousand years old, laughing soundlessly at Harry. Harry wakes up.

NOTE: Dreams Dreams are important in the novel, as they are in psychoanalytic theory, which regards them as expressions of the unconscious, often confusingly masked. In this dream Harry attacks Goethe with the philosophical dilemma that is always on his mind: the struggle between flesh and spirit, mortality and eternity, and how to make life bearable. But in his dream he also finds a recommendation that he is too serious, recalling the advice of the Treatise on humor, and he discovers that Goethe could dance, recalling the bar girl's astonishment that Harry never had learned how. Matthisson and Bürger, whom Harry thinks of in his dream, are two Romantic poets, contemporaries of Goethe. The scorpion with a sting in its tail is one of many crawling creatures that are interpreted in psychoanalytic theory as symbols of sex in dreams and that can simultaneously repel and attract the dreamer.

On waking, since he is still afraid to go home, Harry takes his new friend's advice and sleeps that night at the tavern. He awakes restored and goes home, where his landlady invites him to tea. He relaxes in her respectable, motherly company, and converses humorously on the decline of civilization, a subject about which he would ordinarily be bitter. Harry seems to be taking the advice of the

Treatise (and of Goethe in his dream), and is using humor to make life bearable.

A Taste of Nightlife

The bar girl keeps her dinner date with Harry. She makes him guess her name. He sees in her face the face of his best boyhood friend, whose name was Herman. He guesses that her name is Hermine, the feminine equivalent of Herman. In their further conversation, Hermine tells Harry that he is seeing himself in her, as in a looking glass, but he insists that she is not his reflection but his opposite. Can you think of ways in which both may be true? Remember Jung's theory of the anima, the suppressed female in the male personality which he projects onto the woman in his life.

NOTE: Sex transformations and confusions   Hermine's momentary change into Herman is the first of several male-female transformations that Hermine undergoes. The blurring of the line dividing the sexes, and the argument over whether Hermine is Harry's reflection or his opposite (or both) are significant points in psychoanalytic theory. They may also be elements in Hesse's independent exploration of the unconscious. Sigmund Freud held that it is a creative artist's function to retrieve disturbing symbols like these from the unconscious, and to reveal them in his art. Hesse uses the symbol of sex transformation strikingly in a dream sequence in *Siddhartha*. The combination of both male and female characteristics in an individual is called *hermaphroditism*, from the names of the Greek god

Hermes and the goddess Aphrodite, who had a
hermaphrodite son.

Hermine tells Harry that he will obey all her
commands, including the final command to kill her.
Their conversation, sometimes serious, sometimes
teasing and flirtatious, suddenly verges on sinister
fantasy. It swings back to reality when Hermine
makes plans to give Harry dancing lessons.

At their next meeting, Hermine has found Harry's name in a newspaper story that attacks him
as a pacifist and traitor. She tells him his principles
are worth fighting for, that his life will never be
dull as long as he fights for his beliefs.

NOTE: This argument of Hermine's appealed to
young people in the Sixties. Does it appeal to you?
Would you fight for a cause that had little hope of
victory in your lifetime? Are there any contemporary causes comparable to Haller's pacifism?

Hermine has taught Harry the fox-trot. At a ho-
tel dance, she makes him ask a pretty girl named
Maria to dance with him. The handsome Latin
American saxophonist Pablo comes to their table.
Harry has now met the chief characters of his magic
adventure.

You know how people appear in dreams, recognizable but somehow changed. This soon begins
to happen to Harry. Hermine, Maria, and Pablo
seem real enough up to this point. Maria delights
Harry with her innocent enjoyment of all pleasures, including sex, without guilt. Pablo dresses

flamboyantly, smiles amiably while Harry lectures him about music, and hands Haller a pinch of what must be cocaine to sniff.

Most of all, Hermine seems more than a beautiful bar girl in her understanding of Harry. Hermine and Pablo are already somewhat ambiguous, if not actually magical, figures. Keep your eye on them.

NOTE: Reality and fiction. *Steppenwolf* transforms Hesse's experiences into the imaginary world of fiction. Harry Haller is reliving the author's life at the very time Hesse was writing *Steppenwolf*. Hesse too was struggling out of a crisis of despair, living alone like Haller. He made the rounds of night clubs, eating and drinking and, like Haller, learning to dance. Hesse wrote to a friend that he had finished a course of six lessons: "I do believe that I can master the fox-trot and the one-step to the degree that can be expected of an elderly gentleman suffering from gout." Hesse was still seeing his second wife of a few months, Ruth Wenger, from whom he was separated, but their dates always ended in quarrels and misunderstanding. She is the model for Erika, whose photograph is on Haller's bureau and with whom the nephew saw Haller go out one evening, only to return an hour later, sadder than ever. The model for Hermine was Julia Laubi-Honegger, to whom Hesse wrote letters. The models for Maria and Pablo are not known but were probably people he met in his night life of 1924–26 when he was trying "to become part of the world of ordinary people."

In another of his interior monologues, Harry

muses on the new intrusions in his carefully se-
cluded life. He is tasting pleasures and indulging
some of the many selves that the Treatise and Hermine have told him he has stifled—but he is not
enjoying it. He feels he is a traitor to all he has
held sacred, that his personality is being de-
stroyed. But he goes on. Hermine sends Maria to
teach him the pleasures of sex. He is not surprised
to learn that he is only one of Maria's many men
and that she has been Hermine's lover as well. He
spends his time with Hermine, Maria, and Pablo
in their world of bars, night clubs, and jazz sharing
their pleasures and Pablo's drugs. The climax of
these experiences is the Masked Ball.

Harry confesses to Hermine that he is happy but
is longing for suffering—not the kind he endured
before he met her but a more beautiful suffering
that will make death welcome. She confides that
she, too, has found life a disappointment. The world
had no more use for her gifts than for Harry's ideals.
In her opinion, the great deeds and fine ideas of
heroes and geniuses, as taught in schools, are a
schoolteacher's swindle. Real people have nothing
to look forward to but death and eternity, where
Hermine's saints and Harry's Immortals dwell.

What do you think of Hermine's interpretation
of life? Are the great thoughts and deeds of history
really a swindle, encouraging young people to have
expectations that are never to be fulfilled?

The Masked Ball
Harry has dinner at the old-fashioned tavern, a
shrine to his former lonely life. To pass the hours
until it is time to go to the ball, he drops in on a

movie. It turns out to be the Old Testament epic of Moses leading the Jews out of Egypt.

NOTE: Historical spectacles were among the great achievements of the early silent movies, beginning with D. W. Griffith's *Intolerance* in 1915. The film Harry saw and enjoyed may have been Cecil B. DeMille's *The Ten Commandments* of 1923. Considering Hesse's frequently expressed bias against Americans and American culture, he gives the film, as seen through Harry Haller's eyes, a favorable review here.

Shy and nervous, wearing evening dress rather than a costume, Harry arrives at the ball. He wanders miserably among the revelers, deafened by the noise, lonely in the crowd. Finding no one he knows, he heads for the cloakroom, but he has mislaid the check for his coat. A playful "devil" hands him one, which turns out to be an announcement of the Magic Theater. It says, as before, FOR MADMEN ONLY and NOT FOR EVERYBODY, but adds, PRICE OF ADMITTANCE YOUR MIND and, in a corner, HERMINE IS IN HELL.

Suddenly revived, Harry turns back into the throng, heading for the lower floor decorated as "hell." He finds Maria in Spanish costume and they dance past Pablo who is leading the dance band. He hurries on, to find not Hermine but Herman, the friend of his youth, who turns out to be Hermine dressed as a boy. With Herman/Hermine as his male companion and rival, Harry plunges into the ball. He experiences the intoxicating pleasure of being part of a festive crowd.

People are already leaving when Harry spots a Pierrette, a girl dressed as a clown with a white mask. It is Hermine in a change of costume. Harry is now truly in love with her. She asks, "Are you ready?" Harry is ready. He hears the eerie, icy laughter of the Immortals.

The Magic Theater

Pablo appears, now wearing a gorgeous silk smoking jacket, and invites them into a small room. He offers them an aromatic liquor and long, thin cigarettes. He holds a mirror up to Harry, who sees in it his own face and that of a beautiful, frightened wolf.

NOTE: Readers who have labeled this excursion into the Magic Theater a drug trip have found their evidence here, in Pablo's drinks and cigarettes. Hesse's biographers say with certainty that although Hesse was familiar with drugs as painkillers for his gout and arthritis, he did not participate in the drug culture.

Pablo ushers them into his theater and guides them along a curved passage. It has doors along it like those opening into theater boxes—Pablo calls them his peep shows. He instructs Harry to check his personality in the cloakroom, and again shows him his image with that of the wolf in the little mirror. This time Harry is to destroy it by laughing, by ceasing to take himself seriously. Pablo laughs the eerie laugh Harry heard earlier. Harry himself laughs, and the mirror turns opaque. Pablo throws it away and compliments Harry. He is rid of the Steppenwolf and will soon be free of the farce of reality.

Harry then looks into a gigantic mirror, which shatters into images of himself at all ages. A young Harry leaps from the mirror into Pablo's arms and they go off together. Another, a teenage Harry, also springs out of the mirror and disappears through a door with a sign that reads, ALL GIRLS ARE YOURS—ONE QUARTER IN THE SLOT.

Harry opens a door marked JOLLY HUNTING— GREAT HUNT IN AUTOMOBILES. He is plunged into a war between men and machines, with human bodies and mangled cars strewn in the street. An old schoolfriend named Gustav joins him. Gustav is armed. They drive into the country and climb a tree to a lookout above the road. From there they take turns shooting the drivers of cars passing on the road below. They throw the cars and bodies over the cliff and climb back to shoot the next ones.

The automobile was a symbol of death to Hesse, but here its significance is broadened to embrace all machines, the technology that in Hesse's view is a threat to human values. Do you see modern technology as a threat? Notice that Gustav, a pleasant enough fellow, enjoys killing for its own sake. This is another possible "shadow" in Harry's personality, a potential killer who is suppressed and emerges from the unconscious only in this fantasy.

NOTE: To some readers the automobile hunt labels Hesse as a member of the older generation, hostile to change. Others, young as well as older, remember the frustration of traffic jams and the sensation of being out of control on high-speed freeways, where they sometimes felt like shooting the incompetent and inconsiderate drivers around them. Do you sympathize with this hunt? Can you make a case against the automobile? In your judgment, has modern technology brought more happiness or less to the world?

When the automobile hunt dissolves, Harry finds himself back in the theater corridor. He passes a series of signs promising transformation into a plant or animal, instruction in the Indian arts of love, laughing suicide, wisdom of the East, downfall of the West, a cabinet of humor. He chooses GUIDANCE IN THE BUILDING UP OF THE PERSONALITY. SUCCESS GUARANTEED.

Inside, Harry finds a man sitting on the floor before a chessboard, who looks like Pablo but says he is not anybody. He asks for the pieces of Harry's personality. These are again supplied by a mirror that breaks up Harry's image into pieces about the size of chessmen. The chess player, droning on about multiple selves, demonstrates how the pieces of Harry's personality can be rearranged into various personalities living a series of different lives. Again Hesse introduces the idea of multiple selves, a psychoanalytic approach that first breaks up (analyzes) and then reshapes the different parts of the personality in order to achieve harmony through healthy expression of all the parts.

Fascinated, Harry takes his pieces and withdraws to play his own game, but is interrupted by a sign reading, MARVELOUS TAMING OF THE STEP-PENWOLF. He walks through the door to see a stage like that at a village fair, on which an animal trainer is taming the wolf. Harry is agonized to see the beautiful beast humiliated, but the roles change and under the wolf's commands the man behaves like a wolf, tearing the flesh of his prey. Harry, horrified, flees.

He comes again to the door through which his adolescent self had disappeared: ALL GIRLS ARE YOURS. Here Harry is wafted into his youth and first love, and he relives all the loves of his life that followed, ending with the mirrored image of Hermine. He runs in search of her and comes to the last door, HOW ONE KILLS FOR LOVE. He remembers that to kill Hermine was to be her last command. He looks for the pieces of his personality in order to rearrange them and avoid this outcome. Instead he finds a knife. In the mirror he sees the wolf, larger than life, and then himself. His mirror image tells Harry he is waiting for death.

To music from Mozart's opera, *Don Giovanni*, along with the eerie laughter of an Immortal, Pablo appears in the shape of Mozart. He shows Harry visions of Brahms and Wagner, each leading a crowd of thousands of musicians who played the thousands of extra notes in the music of these composers. It was not their fault, Mozart/Pablo tells Harry. Thick orchestration was a fault of their time. But they must pay the penalty for it all the same. Harry thinks of all the superfluous books, articles, and pamphlets he has written and must be penalized for in an endless purgatory. In anger he seizes Mozart's hair and is whirled away into the icy gaiety of the Immortals until he loses consciousness.

NOTE: Hesse and music   This vision is Hesse's musical joke. Johannes Brahms and Richard Wagner, German composer contemporaries in the late nineteenth century, were considered hostile competitors, and their followers carried on a bitter feud. Both, however, were criticized for the "thickness" of their orchestration—that is, for writing too many notes for too many instruments—compared with the restraint and clarity of their predecessors of the classical period such as Mozart. Brahms used a symphony orchestra much larger than Mozart's, and Wagner added still more instruments to the full orchestra of the time. Other German composers Haller mentions—Franz Schubert and Ludwig van Beethoven, for instance—were pioneers of the post-Mozart Romantic era, which saw innovations of new musical forms and a freer expression of the emotions. Brahms and Wagner came still later, at the climax of the Romantic era; Wagner in particular expressed powerful passions in terms of large orchestral sound. Haller/Hesse grants these late composers some power and beauty but he clings to his worship of Mozart as the greatest of all composers, a true Immortal.

Murder, Execution, and the Verdict

Harry comes to himself in the theater corridor, confronting a mirror in which he looks centuries old. He kicks the mirror into fragments and walks on to yet another door. Within he finds two naked, beautiful figures, Pablo and Hermine, asleep side by side on a rug. Seeing the bruise of a love bite under Hermine's breast, Harry plunges his knife into it. Hermine dies. Pablo wakes, covers her body with the rug, and leaves Harry alone with his deed.

Mozart comes in, now in modern dress, sets up a radio (wireless) and turns it on—it is a broadcast of a composition by George Frederick Handel, yet another German composer and a contemporary of Mozart. Harry protests at being forced to listen to this mechanical distortion of great music. Mozart lectures him: Harry must learn to listen, to hear the divine music being broadcast everywhere. Life is like the radio. Its mechanical "slime" of necessities and vanities comes between the ideal and the real. Harry must learn what is to be taken seriously, and laugh at the rest. This comparison seems to be an effort to make peace with modern technology, conceding that it can enhance experience and does not necessarily destroy art. Do you agree with Mozart's analogy of the radio—its good and bad aspects—with life? Do you think that radio, television, and computers distort experience and art, or do they enhance them? Is it possible to enjoy the machinery of everyday life on its own merits without comparing it to some ideal?

But Harry must now pay the price of murder. He finds himself in a prison yard, facing a jury in formal morning dress. The prosecutor reads the charge and Harry kneels before the guillotine. Instead of the death penalty, he is condemned to eternal life and is laughed out of court. The jury bursts into otherworldly laughter and Harry comes to himself again, with Mozart beside him.

The charges against Harry are three: He stabbed a reflection of a girl with a reflection of a knife. He used the Magic Theater as a way of achieving suicide. Lastly, he is lacking in humor.

Mozart teases him for his "romantics." Harry is ready to suffer death as an atonement—he is willing to die but not to live. Mozart offers to restore Hermine to life and make her Harry's wife. Harry declines—he is not ready and it would result in unhappiness. He protests against Mozart's interference in his life. Mozart offers him one of his cigarettes and is suddenly transformed back into Pablo.

Pablo says he is disappointed in Harry for spattering the Magic Theater's picture world with reality. He picks up Hermine, now a miniature figurine, and puts her in his pocket. The show is over. Harry, weary and ready for sleep, is willing to begin the game of life anew. He will suffer its tortures and will journey through the hell of his inner self not once but as often as necessary.

The conversation with Mozart/Pablo contains the final message of *Steppenwolf*: one must learn not to die but to live, even though to live is harder.

In the end, Harry agrees to live. He will become better at the game. He will make the exploratory journey into his inner self again and again, painful though it is, as often as necessary. Pablo and Mozart are both waiting for him—meaning that he may no longer suffer from his terrible solitude, that from now on he may be able to enjoy Pablo's world of pleasure as well as Mozart's world of art.

And so the book ends, with no real conclusion but with a promise for Harry's happier future.

NOTE: Hesse's "postscript" to the novel For Hesse, the future did indeed turn out happier than his and Harry's past. Hesse married for the third time in 1931, and this time it proved successful. In 1941 Hesse wrote a "Postscript to *Steppenwolf*" (reprinted as an "Author's Note—1961" in some editions).

In this postscript, Hesse points out that of all his books, *Steppenwolf* was the one most often and violently misunderstood. Usually, though, those who misinterpreted it were not those who rejected it but its most enthusiastic readers, and not only young readers but those of his own age, who identified themselves with Harry Haller and shared Haller's griefs and struggles. These readers, Hesse says, found *Steppenwolf* a novel of despair.

This is incorrect, he says. The novel is also about a higher, indestructible world beyond the Steppenwolf, a world of the spirit, the arts, and "the immortal men who oppose the Steppenwolf's world of suffering with a positive, serene, super-personal and timeless world of faith." The note ends with Hesse's acknowledgment that the novel pictures a disease and a crisis, but he claims that it leads to healing, not death.

This was the author's interpretation of his novel fifteen years after he wrote it, when his own life had changed from one of chaos and pain to harmony and happiness. Can you make a case either for or against his opinion of the novel's message?

Consider this further question: Does an author have a particular right to explain the meaning of his work? Some might say that the work should speak for itself, that if the author feels the need to explain it the novel has failed. A counterargument might be that the author has at least the same right as anyone else, critic or public, to argue the meaning of the novel, and that *Steppenwolf* is subtle enough, perhaps even ambiguous enough, to arouse disagreements as to its interpretation. Which side of this argument would you take?

A STEP BEYOND

Test and Answers
TEST

1. Harry Haller acquires the "Treatise on the Steppenwolf" by _____
   A. buying it in a bookstore
   B. picking it up in the street
   C. having it handed to him by a peddler

2. The first-person narrator of the Preface is _____
   A. the editor of Hesse's collected works
   B. the landlady's nephew
   C. Hermann Hesse

3. The Immortals in *Steppenwolf* are _____
   A. great creative artists
   B. world conquerors
   C. founders of the major religions

4. Hermine's last command to Harry is to _____
   A. marry her   B. kill her
   C. make love to her

5. The automobile hunt represents the _____
   A. bloodthirstiness of Harry's wolf personality
   B. violence suggested at the Masked Ball
   C. war of man against the machine

6. The shattering of Harry's mirror image means _____

A. the breakup of Harry's personality
   into its many selves
B. Harry's self-hatred
C. Harry's wolf self is forever gone

7. When Harry goes on trial, he is condemned   _____
   to
   A. exile   B. death   C. life

8. To reconcile Harry with life, the Treatise   _____
   prescribes
   A. drugs   B. humor   C. suicide

9. Pablo rebukes Harry for   _____
   A. refusing his drugs
   B. not dancing to his music
   C. spoiling his pictures with reality

10. Before entering the Magic Theater, Pablo   _____
    asks Harry to
    A. take off his shoes
    B. check his personality in the cloakroom
    C. swear not to tell anyone what he sees

11. Hermann Hesse said that *Steppenwolf* was his ca-
    tharsis. What does the word mean, and how might
    the novel serve that purpose?

12. *Steppenwolf* has been described as a psychoanalytic
    novel. Identify and explain some of the psychoan-
    alytic symbols in the novel.

13. Harry Haller despises the middle class but chooses
    to live in middle-class surroundings. How does he
    reveal this contradiction and how is it explained?

14. *Steppenwolf* is structured as a "framework" novel.
    Describe the form. What is its literary purpose?

ANSWERS

1. C	2. B	3. A	4. B	5. C	6. A
7. C	8. B	9. C	10. B		

11. Catharsis is a word of Greek origin meaning a cleansing or purging. It came to mean the effect of a work of art in cleansing the emotions, removing what is painful or destructive in them by giving them expression in an art form. This principle was voiced by the Greek philosopher Aristotle in the fourth century B.C. Hermann Hesse was in a deeply depressed state when he began to write *Steppenwolf*, and it became his most autobiographical novel. In it he transferred his psychological distress and his experiences with people and events first into his central character, Harry Haller, and then into Harry's fantasy experiences in the Magic Theater. In this way both the fictional Harry and the author Hesse achieved release from their emotional suffering. In the novel, Harry resolves to go on and learn to live better. Hesse recovered from his depression and within a few years entered into his third marriage, which proved successful.

12. While Hesse did not identify psychoanalytic symbols in his novel, readers have interpreted them and given them the technical names they have in psychoanalytic theory. The wolf of the steppes, Harry's second self, is seen as the "shadow" in the theory according to Carl Gustav Jung. This is the side of an individual's personality that is unacceptable to his conscious self and is therefore suppressed. Hermine is interpreted as Harry's "anima," in Jungian theory the feminine side of the male individual, which he suppresses as an unacceptable weakness and may project onto his wife or mistress, as Harry projects his anima onto Hermine. The shattering of Harry's mirrored image into many pieces represents the breaking up of the personality into its multiple aspects, to be reshaped into better harmony by psychoanalysis. Magic, as in the Magic Theater, is identified in Jungian theory with the unconscious. The automobile in Harry's fantasy hunt is a symbol of death. Harry's obsession with death—suicide, murder, execution—in one interpretation is a longing to escape from the necessity of confronting one's unconscious. Hermann Hesse was familiar with the work of Sigmund Freud and underwent psychoanalysis with a pupil of Freud's Swiss disciple, Jung, who formulated his own psychoanalytic system.

13. Harry Haller in his interior monologues repeatedly expresses his disgust with the bourgeoisie, or middle class, for its materialism, its planned avoidance of extremes of feeling, and its orderly way of life. Yet he chooses middle-class lodgings. He enjoys the smell of furniture polish and floor wax in his landlady's hallway, and he makes a kind of temple out of the foyer with its immaculate potted plants. The Treatise analyzes this contradiction as stemming from Harry's middle-class upbringing, from which he has never been able to escape. Harry himself recognizes it as a kind of homesickness for the setting of his childhood. He sadly realizes that he can never recapture that lost home, but also that he cannot accept its values and so must always be in conflict.

14. A "framework" novel is one introduced by an apparently realistic preface to an unrealistic memoir. Hesse used this structure in *Demian* in 1919 and *The Glass Bead Game* in 1943, as well as in *Steppenwolf* in 1927. Its literary function is to give a commonsense introduction, by an observer, to a narrative that may be a fantasy. In *Steppenwolf* the Preface is by a conventional neighbor of Harry

Haller. This narrator's description of Harry as a real though eccentric individual lends solidity to Harry as a character and contributes to the credibility of the fantastic experiences that Harry himself narrates. As a literary device, the framework offers a dramatic contrast for the body of the novel.

Glossary

FOR *STEPPENWOLF*

Anima Feminine counterpart of the male personality in Jungian psychoanalytic theory.

Archetype Mythical image in the collective unconscious (Jungian theory) such as the Mother or the Wise Old Man.

Bach, Friedemann German composer, eldest son of J. S. Bach, 1710–84, a contemporary of Mozart.

Bach, Johann Sebastian German composer, 1685–1750, the master of his time and one of the great men of music.

Baudelaire, Charles French poet, 1821–1867; also a critic and translator of the American Edgar Allen Poe.

Bürger, Gottfried August German poet, 1747–1794, of the Romantic era.

Catharsis Cleansing or purging of destructive emotions by art.

Freud, Sigmund Austrian physician, founder of psychoanalysis, 1856–1939.

Goethe, Johann Wolfgang von German poet, playwright, novelist, 1749–1832.

Hermaphrodite Individual having both male and female characteristics.

Jean Paul Pen name of Johann Paul Friedrich Richter, German author, 1763–1825, of the Romantic era.

Jung, Carl Gustav Swiss physician and psychoanalyst,

1875–1961, who broke with Freud to formulate his own theory.

Matthisson, Friedrich von   German poet, 1761–1831, of the Romantic era.

Molly   Character in a German Romantic poem.

Mozart, Wolfgang Amadeus   Austrian composer, 1756–1791, greatest of his time, the "classical" or pre-Romantic era.

Nietzsche, Friedrich Wilhelm   German philosopher, 1844–1900, known for his concept of the "superman."

Novalis   Pen name of Friedrich von Hardenberg, German author, 1772–1801, a leader of Romanticism.

Persona   Public image or mask of the personality, according to Jungian theory.

Pietism   Fundamentalist sect of the Lutheran Church that made the Bible a daily guide and forbade dancing, theater, and sports. Hesse's parents were Pietists.

Shadow   Aspect of the personality, usually suppressed, according to Jungian theory.

Stifter, Adalbert   Austrian author who had a fatal accident while shaving, 1805–1868.

Transvestite   Person who wears clothing of the opposite sex.

Siddhartha

THE NOVEL

Religious Background: Hinduism and Buddhism

Siddhartha, an Indian Poem is the title Hermann Hesse gave to his story of an Indian prince in search of an understanding of his life. As a Brahmin, a member of the highest and most spiritual caste, Siddhartha is born to Hindu priesthood. While in his search, he meets the founder of Buddhism. Thus, an acquaintance with both these major Eastern religions is important to your understanding of the novel.

About 3,500 years ago (1500 B.C.) a nomadic Asian people invaded India from the northwest and settled there. They called themselves Aryans, meaning "noble," and they brought with them their language, Sanskrit, their nature gods, and their traditional literature, the Vedas, a collection of Sanskrit hymns and prayers which are the nucleus of Hinduism. In time, a more formal priestly religion called Brahmanism, with a strict system of

social classes or castes, replaced the simpler early
religion. The Upanishads, commentaries on the
Vedas and on the nature of reality, were a later
addition to the Hindu scripture. These writings
teach the existence of a universal soul with which
individual souls are united when they conquer the
illusion of time and space, called Maya. Otherwise
a soul must follow its Karma, or fate, through various lives, animal as well as human, paying for evils
committed in former incarnations.

Buddhism arose in the fifth century B.C. as a
reform religion, offering a more personal and individual expression than the fixed Hindu rituals of
cleansings, prayers, sacrifices, pilgrimages to sacred places, and bathing in sacred rivers such as
the Ganges. Its founder was a historical person-
age, a Prince Siddhartha (not the same as the novel's hero) who left his young family and a life of
luxury to seek an escape from suffering for humanity. Enlightenment came to him as he medi-
tated under a bo tree, and he went on to teach that
to free oneself from all ties of love and desire was
the path to Nirvana (literally, nothingness), meaning the escape from the cycle of endless rebirths.
His followers named him the Buddha, the Enlightened One, and his teachings began to be written
down in the year of his death, 483 B.C., as the Pali
scripture. Pali is a dialect of Sanskrit, thought to
have been the Buddha's native speech. Buddhism
reached its peak in India during the reign of Asoka
and his son Mahendra, enlightened monarchs of
the third century B.C. Although Buddhism did not
survive as a major Indian religion, Buddhist monks
spread their teachings to China and Japan, where
they took root.

The Buddha taught the Four Noble Truths and the Eightfold Path. The four truths are: existence is suffering, suffering arises from desire, suffering ends when desire ends, and the way to end desire is to follow the eightfold path. The Eightfold Path consists of: right belief, right resolve, right speech, right conduct, right occupation, right effort, right contemplation, and right ecstasy. These rules made Buddhism an "ethical" religion, and its promise of release into eternal bliss also made it a "salvation" religion. Hinduism developed later forms that embodied some of these principles and also promised "salvation," meaning liberation from worldly suffering. One of the later Hindu teachings was yoga, a system of physical and spiritual exercises to hasten salvation, the reunion of the individual soul with the universal soul.

The Plot

Siddhartha, a beautiful youth of princely birth, has studied the teachings and rituals of the Hindu religion. His father, a devout member of the priestly Brahmin caste, expects his son to become a teacher, priest, and princely Brahmin like himself. But Siddhartha is not satisfied with this life-style, and after besting his father in a clash of wills he leaves home to join the Samanas. These are wandering religious men who seek release from the cycle of life by meditation and the practice of asceticism, or extreme self-denial. His boyhood friend Govinda goes with him.

After three years with the Samanas in the forest, Siddhartha decides that theirs is not the way to understanding either. He and Govinda go to Gotama (or Gautama) Buddha, a famous holy man who is preaching nearby. Siddhartha converses with the Buddha, who smiles as one who has achieved the bliss of escape from life's desires and its sufferings. Although deeply impressed, Siddhartha decides to go on and find his own way. The two friends part when Govinda chooses to join the Buddha's monks.

Siddhartha realizes that he has now cast off all ties with family and friends, all reliance on teachers and teachings, and must begin life anew like one newly born. For the first time, he experiences the natural world in all its beauty.

He sleeps in a ferryman's hut and crosses the river. He approaches Kamala, a beautiful courtesan who will teach him the arts of love if he comes richly dressed and bearing gifts. To win Kamala, Siddhartha enters the business world of the merchant Kamaswami. He becomes rich and powerful, but as the years pass he is entrapped in the world of material things. He is so sickened that he finally abandons his wealth and possessions—and Kamala—and leaves the city.

On the riverbank again, he comes close to committing suicide. He falls into a deep sleep, and awakens to find Govinda, in his monk's garb, watching over him. They part a second time, Govinda to continue on his Buddhist way, Siddhartha to recross the river. Siddhartha finds Vasudeva, the gentle ferryman of his previous crossing, and remains as his helper, living simply and learning what the river teaches.

Kamala arrives on a pilgrimage to Gotama Buddha, who is dying. With her is Siddhartha's son, born after Siddhartha left her. Kamala is bitten by a snake and dies, and the boy, now eleven, remains.

Siddhartha now experiences what he never felt before: love and the pain of love for his son. The boy is angry, rebellious, scornful of his father's menial calling and simple way of life, and he runs away. Siddhartha follows him, but turns back as Vasudeva urges him to do.

By the river again, Siddhartha learns from the flowing water the ultimate wisdoms: that time does not exist, that all things in the world are part of a single unity, and that the way to peace is through love. Vasudeva leaves him, disappearing into the forest. Govinda at last comes by again, to discover in the aged Siddhartha a smiling, radiant, holy man.

The Characters

Siddhartha

The name means "he who attains his goal" or "he who is on the right road." It was the given name of the historical Gotama (or Gautama) Buddha of the sixth century B.C., who founded Buddhism. Although the hero of Hesse's novel has the same name and follows a somewhat parallel course, he is a fictional character. (Hesse never explained why he chose the Buddha's name for his hero.)

Like the historical Buddha, Hesse's Siddhartha is a young prince who leaves home and family to seek enlightenment. Although surrounded by love and luxury, and instilled with Hindu learning, he is already certain that he cannot achieve his goal by this route. The trait that drives him along his

course is his independence of mind. He is con-
vinced that no teacher, not even the illustrious Gotama Buddha, can communicate the ultimate wisdom—that it cannot be taught but must be
experienced.

Siddhartha displays qualities of self-discipline and
self-reliance. He is even so bold and self-assured
as to argue about the logic of the Buddha's teaching with the Buddha himself. Siddhartha feels
himself superior to the "child-people," the ordinary folk around him; humility is not part of his
character at the beginning of his quest. Some readers interpret this as the self-confidence of youth;
others see it as arrogance, a character defect. What's
your opinion?

As it turns out, Siddhartha is not superior to
ordinary folk in at least one respect. Although he
enters the world of business and sensual pleasure
as a game, he becomes trapped in it like the people
he scorns.

Kamala, the beautiful courtesan, tells him that,
like herself, he is incapable of love. He does finally
experience love as an old man. Yet it is through
love and its pain, which he overcomes, that he at
last achieves wisdom.

Siddhartha's Father
This princely Brahmin, a member of the highest
Hindu caste, is an example to Siddhartha of learning and devoutness. In a test of wills, the father is
forced to bow to his son's powerful determination
to leave home. As they part, he asks his son to tell
him the secret of bliss when he finds it. This is a
poignant confession for so devout a Brahmin to

make: even after a lifetime of sacrifice, prayer, and
cleansing ablutions, he has not found peace.

Govinda

Siddhartha's boyhood friend and companion is also
a seeker after wisdom, but he is content to learn
from teachers and remain a follower. His name
means "keeper of cows," and because cows are
sacred in Hinduism, this suggests a religious calling. Govinda leaves Siddhartha to become a
Buddhist monk, but like Siddhartha's father he fails
to find peace by his chosen path.

The Samanas

These wandering ascetics are members of a sect
that believes in achieving liberation from the self
through extreme self-denial. They live as wandering beggars without shelter, all but naked, indif-
ferent to rain, cold, or hunger, and given to long
periods of sitting immobile in meditation.

Gotama Buddha

The founder of Buddhism has a radiant, smiling
face that Siddhartha recognizes at once as holy,
although he has never before seen the celebrated
teacher. The Buddha's teaching calls for freeing
oneself from all attachments and desires in order
to escape from the sufferings of life. In his brief
appearance in the novel he is a perfect example of
blissful detachment. But perhaps he isn't all that
detached. Is there a hint that although he listens
courteously, young Siddhartha's argument that
there is a crack in the Buddha's logic may have
stung him? Otherwise, why would he warn this
youth, a complete stranger, not to be too clever?

Kamala

The *kama* of this courtesan's name means physical love, an aspect of the material and sensual world. When written with a capital, as Kama, it is the Hindu god of desire. On the surface Kamala is a worldly woman who will accept Siddhartha only when he comes well dressed and bringing gifts. On a deeper level, she too is a seeker. She gives her pleasure garden to the Buddha and his monks, and at the end she undertakes her final journey to pay him honor on his deathbed. She admits that she is unable to feel love, and she observes this same deficiency in Siddhartha.

Kamaswami

The merchant who takes Siddhartha into his business has a name that means master (*swami*) of the material world (again, *kama*). But it soon becomes clear that although he is successful and wealthy, he is not in fact the master but the slave of his business, driven by the need to succeed and the fear of failure. What could this forecast for Siddhartha? Do you see similarities with the typical American dream of success?

Vasudeva

The kindly ferryman turns out to be the teacher who, simply by listening, points the way to wisdom for Siddhartha. He speaks little but when he does he utters wise counsel. When he leaves Siddhartha, he goes in godlike fashion, not dying but simply disappearing into the woods. He is in fact a god: his name means "one who abides in all

things and in whom all things abide." His name
is one of the names of Krishna, an earthly incarnation of the Hindu god Vishnu the Preserver.

Little Siddhartha

Siddhartha's son has been brought up in Kamala's
house in wealth and luxury. He is a spoiled child,
angry and rebellious. He is impatient with his father,
a stranger to him, and contemptuous of the simple
life on the riverbank. He finally runs away to the
city. Do you see any of Siddhartha's character traits
in this boy? What might redirect the son to a search
for enlightenment?

Other Elements

SETTING

Siddhartha's journey takes him through India,
but it is an India of an ancient era or perhaps not
of any historic era. This India may never have
existed except in Hesse's imagination. It is a
landscape stripped down to its symbolic elements: a palace, a forest, a grove where a sage—
or a magician?—rules over his followers, a pleasure garden whose mistress is a beautiful temp-
tress, a city where fortunes are made and where
men eat, drink, gamble, and indulge in all pleasures. Finally there is the river, with the ferryman's simple hut and his small rice field. Do these
elements remind you of any familiar setting?
Could you describe this setting in terms of the
classic fairy tale?

First comes the palace of tradition, Siddhartha's

father's house. Next is the forest of ordeals to be
braved and conquered, the sojourn with the Samanas, and then the magician in the grove, the
Buddha, pointing out a different path. After that
comes the garden of sensual pleasures, and the
city of material rewards and exciting entertainments. And between the palace, forest, and grove
on one side, and the beautiful woman's garden
and the glittering city on the other, flows the river.
The river is first the dividing line between the spiritual and the material realms through which Siddhartha pursues his quest, and then it becomes
the path to understanding the unity of all experience.

A second interpretation of the novel is as an allegory, one perhaps comparable to the seventeenth-century Christian classic, *The Pilgrim's
Progress.* An allegory is a story whose characters
and settings stand for moral or spiritual ideas. The
meanings of the characters' names in *Siddhartha* are
part of the book's allegorical form. The setting as
well is filled with morally perilous and seductive
places that the hero must negotiate in order to find
its spiritual center.

The narrative stops only once for a physical description of the setting. Siddhartha is leaving the
spiritual side of the river when he discovers the
natural world around him, seeing it in all its beauty
and diversity. Hindu teaching has instructed him
to ignore the physical world as a transient and
meaningless illusion. His discovery that it has
meaning is a significant step in his journey toward
understanding, and this is the reason it is given
such detailed description.

THEMES

1. A QUEST

Myths, legends, and sagas of different peoples follow the theme of a hero's quest—for a precious object, such as the Holy Grail sought by King Arthur's knights, for heavenly salvation, or, as in the case of Siddhartha, for some great truth. He sets out to find the bliss of perfect understanding and unity with Atman, the creator and center of the universe. One after another he tries and abandons the religious ways that are offered to him, and then experiences the world of pleasure and the senses. He achieves his goal, but only by steps. The first step is when he discovers that it is the world of creation—nature itself—that he must understand and embrace. The next step is his realization that it is he, himself, whom he has been trying to escape, but whom instead he must learn to know. And when at last he follows the teaching of the river, he finds a way known to hermits and mystics of all the great religions both Eastern and Western: the path to wisdom and unity with the world that lies through the patient exploration of the self. What do you think the river is really telling Siddhartha? Is it that after he has experienced everything else in life, the only thing left to explore is his own inner world?

2. THE DISCOVERY OF LOVE

After leading Siddhartha through the great Eastern religions of Brahministic Hinduism, Samana asceticism, and finally Buddhism, Hesse at last gives him one element that belongs to no Eastern religion but is at the foundation of Western Christian

belief: the element of love. Siddhartha has envied
the "child-people," the ordinary folk around him,
their feelings of love—for each other, for their children, for themselves and their aspirations. He acknowledges with Kamala that he himself cannot
love, although Kamala is dear to him. But love
comes to him at the end, as a very painful love for
his son, who does not return it but runs away.
Listening to the river, Siddhartha learns to accept
both the pain of love and its loss. One of the images that teach him reconciliation is that of his
father, who had also loved and lost a son—Siddhartha himself. At the end, Siddhartha attempts
for Govinda's sake to reconcile his belief in the
importance of love with the Buddha's rejection of
love. Do you find his argument convincing?

3.   AN AUTOBIOGRAPHY
Hesse wrote that all his books were in some way
autobiographical, and *Siddhartha* can be interpreted as autobiography thinly screened. In it Hesse
revisits an India that, as he hinted elsewhere, never
existed in reality even in ancient times, but it was
the India he imagined, in his childhood, in his parents' house filled with Indian artifacts and in the
picture books about India in his grandfather's library. As in a dream, all the features of this landscape have symbolic meaning, as do its characters.
They are the figures that dominated Hesse's childhood. Siddhartha's father and the learned Brahmins represent Hesse's father and his fellow missionaries, and the Brahministic rituals symbolize
the stern commands and prohibitions of their Pietist faith. Siddhartha's struggle of will with his father
and his eventual escape into the forest are Hesse's

escape from his parents' expectations. Like Siddhartha's flight into the Samana struggle with the
self, Hesse's flight led him into a lifelong struggle
with his bourgeois background and his artistic self.
Can you follow Hesse's life through Siddhartha's
quest? Siddhartha's immersion in the world of the
senses and pleasures was also Hesse's. The intense self-exploration by the river might be compared with Hesse's psychoanalytic experience,
substituting Vasudeva (the wise old man) for the
psychoanalyst. That Hesse's life story is set in a
dreamlike Indian landscape and told through Indian characters is seen as one of Hesse's artistic
triumphs. *Siddhartha* is considered by a number of
Hesse scholars as his most perfect novel.

4. FINDING ONE'S OWN WAY

Siddhartha rejects first the Brahministic teachings of his father, then the self-denying practices
of the Samanas, and finally the teachings of the
Buddha, greatest of all teachers. At this point Siddhartha has rejected all teaching, believing that one
must find one's own way. Knowledge can be
taught, but not wisdom, he says. He notes that
the Buddha achieved his blissful understanding not
through any teaching but by way of his own patient search. Accordingly, the Buddha's teachings
contain all the knowledge necessary for living a
good life, but omit the secret of enlightenment,
which can only be experienced, not taught. So Siddhartha goes on alone. He discovers the beauty of
nature, which in Hindu belief must be ignored because it is Maya, illusion. In Christian teaching,
the world and everything in it is God's creation
and therefore to be embraced and respected. But

this also suggests the unity of all things, which is
a Hindu concept, and the All of Buddhism, so that
Siddhartha's discovery of the natural world may
be a first step toward the wisdom that all life is
one.

5. THE RIVER

In eight of the twelve chapters of *Siddhartha* a
clear boundary is drawn between the spiritual and
the material worlds: the river. When Siddhartha
crosses it, he leaves on one side the Brahmins, the
Samanas, the Buddhists—all aspects of the religious and spiritual. On the other side he plunges
into the business world of the merchant Kamaswami, the sensuous world of the courtesan Kamala, and the physical luxuries and pleasures of
city life. He savors all this for twenty years, and
then suddenly turns away and returns to the river.
Here he shares the simple life of Vasudeva the
ferryman, and for the next twenty years listens to
the river. The river is no longer a boundary that
divides. Now it represents a unity in which past,
present, and future, all people and their experiences, all aspects of life flow together. Siddhartha
comes to understand that there is no conflict between the spiritual and the material, that all human experience is to be embraced, and that the
only difference between ordinary people and sages
is that the sages understand this unity. This is the
vision that Siddhartha at last sees in the river.

STYLE

In harmony with his hero's quest through ancient religions and scenes of imagined antiquity,

the story of *Siddhartha* is told in the style of an ancient saga or epic. The language has been compared with translations from the Sanskrit and Pali languages of the Hindu and Buddhist scriptures. Hermann Hesse read these translated texts when he undertook intensive studies in Indian religious literature during his psychoanalysis. An influence more familiar to Hesse's Western readers is the Bible, which was central to the daily life of the pious Christian household of Hesse's childhood.

All three of these sources share the qualities of a literature that was passed on by word of mouth for centuries before it was written down. You will find here the singing rhythms, the repetition of phrases, and the poetic chants and prayers of storytellers and preachers. Most listeners in ancient times were illiterate, and the rhythmic language and repetitious patterns of sentence structure were aids to memory.

These stylistic devices had another effect, that of a dreamlike, almost hypnotic experience for their listeners. For English-speaking readers the closest approximation of this style is the King James Version of the Bible. Try reading some passages from *Siddhartha* aloud and see—or rather, hear—for yourself the trancelike and yet deeply moving rhythms of the work. The translation by Hilda Rosner, first published in 1951 (New Directions), was widely praised for its fidelity to the original and for its beauty. Can you identify the stylistic elements that make it poetic and song-like? Consider these few sentences from the passage in which Siddhartha discovers the natural world:

All this had always been and he had never seen
it; he was never present. Now he was present
and belonged to it. Through his eyes he saw
light and shadows; through his mind he was
aware of moon and stars.

And this, with its triple phrasing:

. . . and the river's voice was full of longing,
full of smarting woe, full of insatiable desire.

Another quality appears in the dialogues between Siddhartha and the merchant Kamaswami,
notably in the job interview. The speech is simple
and direct, but it has elements of the riddles posed
in ancient legends, to which the hero always has
a ready answer. It also recalls the debates of learned
religious men who discuss and analyze the meaning of each word and phrase in the scriptures—
like the rabbis in their commentaries on the Old
Testament, the Talmud. The Hindu scriptures also
had their volumes of commentaries, the Upanishads. Note the riddle-like questions and answers
in Siddhartha's conversations with Kamaswami, and
the argument that Siddhartha presents to the Buddha in the grove.

POINT OF VIEW

The story of *Siddhartha* is told by a third-person
omniscient narrator who stands outside the story
but occasionally enters into the mind of a character
to tell what he or she is thinking. Most often it is
Siddhartha's thoughts and feelings that are described, and how others appear to him, so that the
focus of the novel is primarily on its main character. There are occasions when that focus shifts,

as, for example, at the beginning, when the attitudes of the palace household are described, and later in the brief references to how Kamaswami and Kamala react to Siddhartha's disappearance. Another shift away from Siddhartha occurs when the narrator looks out through the dying Kamala's eyes as she recognizes her former lover, Siddhartha, and finds in him the peace she had hoped to obtain from the Buddha. The final chapter, entitled "Govinda," focuses on Siddhartha's boyhood friend when they meet again in old age at the river bank. It is through Govinda's eyes that the narrator gives you a final picture of the Siddhartha who has achieved the goal of his quest.

FORM AND STRUCTURE

The story of *Siddhartha* is told in a straightforward, chronological form. It follows the hero from his princely youth through a series of spiritual and worldly adventures until he achieves his goal of peace and understanding. The form is biographical, but it is also an allegory in which the characters represent the qualities that their names signify. The hero's experiences, although told as real events, can also be seen as a symbolic inner quest. In its progression from one episode to another *Siddhartha* has also been compared with the sagas of legendary heroes.

The story is divided into two unequal parts of four chapters in Part One and eight in Part Two. Part One takes Siddhartha from his father's house, through the years with the Samanas and the encounter with the Buddha, to the "Awakening" in which Siddhartha breaks all ties with the past and goes forward alone. Part Two takes him across the river, and in the first four chapters of this section he experiences sensual love, financial success, and the worldly life of the city. Realizing at last that he is trapped, he leaves all this and returns to the river. In the fourth of these chapters he reaches his lowest point of despair and begins to recover. In the next chapter he recrosses the river and remains there through the remaining chapters, living the simple life and achieving at last the peace of a holy man. Although they are not formally separated into a third part, the last four chapters of Siddhartha's life on the river can be viewed as a third part of the story.

Some readers have interpreted this three-part structure as a triad representing Innocence, Guilt, and Redemption. Another version of the three-part structure is in terms of thesis, antithesis, and synthesis. The thesis and antithesis are opposites—in this case spiritual life versus a worldly and sensual existence—and the synthesis is the conclusion that embodies harmonious aspects of both—Siddhartha's acceptance of the unity of all creation.

Although the novel follows a straight chronological line without flashbacks or digressions, its handling of time is not precise. The three years with the Samanas and the twenty years with Kamala and in the city go by uncounted. You learn only afterward how much time has elapsed. Each of the three parts has covered twenty years of Siddhartha's life.

The author's formal division of the book into two parts—of four and eight chapters, respectively—suggests to some readers that Hesse intended to symbolize the Four Noble Truths and the Eightfold Path as taught by the Buddha. In the opinion of others this seems unlikely, considering Siddhartha's ultimate rejection of Buddha's teaching.

The Story

PART ONE

THE BRAHMIN'S SON

"In the shade of the house, in the sunshine on the river by the boats, in the shade of the sallow wood and the fig tree . . ." are the opening lines that set the poetic tone of the novel. Hesse called the novel "an Indian poem" and although it is written in prose it begins with the dreamlike musical rhythm of an epic poem.

NOTE: The sallow wood is an Old World willow. The American epic poems of Henry Wadsworth Longfellow begin in a similar way. "This is the forest primeval, the murmuring pines and the hemlocks" is the first line of *Evangeline*. "By the shores of Gitche Gumee,/ By the shining Big-Sea-Water" are the first two lines of *Hiawatha's Childhood*.

The story describes Siddhartha's beauty and grace, how beloved he is in his father's palace, and how well he has kept up with the religious teachings and rituals of the priestly Brahmin caste into which he was born. Siddhartha gives joy to every-

one but is not himself joyful. The Brahmins of his
father's court have poured all their learning into
him, yet he is filled with unanswered questions.

NOTE: Castes   Hindu society, according to traditional precepts, is divided into a hierarchy of four
classes, or castes, each having a special social function.

At the top are the Brahmins who are considered
as spiritually pure by virtue of their birth into the
caste. As such, they perform the priestly, religious
function. Next come the nobility, called Vsatriyas,
who are the warriors and whose role it is to defend
society. Commerce and farming belong to the third
group, the Vaisyas, who are followed by the fourth,
and lowest caste, the Sudras, or servants. (It is
from the fourth caste that the even lower subclass
of so-called "untouchables" is drawn. They perform the duties considered too impure for any
Hindu to do, such as tending to corpses and clean-
ing away human and animal wastes.)

Membership in a caste is by inheritance, and,
although a man's profession is no longer fixed by
caste, his status usually is.

Why worship gods? They were, after all, created
forms, mortal and transient like human beings.
Where can Atman, the Universal Soul, be found?
Siddhartha tells his friend Govinda that he will
leave his father's house and join the Samanas. To
exact his father's permission to leave, Siddhartha
stands waiting silently through the night. At last
his father gives in, asking Siddhartha in parting to

come back and teach him the way to bliss if he finds it.

This is a poignant admission from the devout Brahmin. With all the ritual cleansings, prayers, and sacrifices, is he still seeking bliss? Is he, like Siddhartha, also plagued by doubts? This surely strengthens Siddhartha's rejection of the orthodox Brahminic Hinduism.

Siddhartha and Govinda leave together.

NOTE: Some readers see Govinda as Siddhartha's psychoanalytic "shadow," the conflicting and therefore suppressed aspect of the personality, according to the theories of Carl Gustav Jung. (See page 19.) In *Steppenwolf*, Harry Haller's shadow was the part of himself he called a wolf. What evidence can you find to support the interpretation of Govinda as another side of Siddhartha?

WITH THE SAMANAS

Siddhartha gives away his fine clothes, keeping only a loincloth and a rough cloak. He learns to fast and to endure heat, cold, hunger, and pain. He masters the control of his breathing and heartbeat. He learns to slip out of the consciousness of himself into other creatures, experiencing the life cycle in which the soul migrates endlessly from one life form into another. His goal is to become empty of the Self and so reach the secret of pure Being.

NOTE: Holy men of India are celebrated for their ability to mentally control even unconscious bodily functions like bleeding and burning. Some of these effects have been accomplished in the West through use of hypnosis.

Disappointingly, Siddhartha always finds himself returning to consciousness of the Self. Govinda praises him for learning the exercises so quickly. But Siddhartha tells him that anyone can achieve the same results with wine and a prostitute at a tavern. The oldest Samana has been practicing the exercises for years and has still not achieved bliss.

Amid rumors of a great teacher, Gotama Buddha, the two youths decide to go and hear him. Their old Samana teacher scolds them for leaving, but Siddhartha subdues him with an exercise of hypnotic power, and they leave. What do you think of this demonstration by Siddhartha? Some readers find it an arrogant display of power at the expense of an old man's dignity. Do you think that Siddhartha, with all his gifts, may be guilty of conceit? Are there other instances of this in his behavior?

GOTAMA

The Buddha is one of many monks in identical yellow robes, but Siddhartha knows him at once for the holy man. The two youths listen to the Buddha's teaching, and Govinda decides to stay and join the Buddha's followers. Since Siddhartha will not do this, the friends part.

Siddhartha meets the Buddha walking in the grove and engages him in discussion. Siddhartha singles out a flaw in the Buddha's teaching: that by following his path, others can also achieve the same release from the pain of life. Siddhartha contends that the Buddha reached bliss not through teaching but alone and in his own way. Siddhartha believes that wisdom cannot be taught—that it can only be achieved by experience. That is why he will not stay as one of the Buddha's followers. Friendly and courteous, the Buddha dismisses him with a warning against being too clever.

Would you add this incident of lecturing the Buddha to the display of hypnotic power in the previous chapter? Siddhartha's gifts certainly do not include humility! And what do you think of the Buddha's warning to Siddhartha not to be too clever? Is it possible that this arrogant argument from a youthful debater has dented the great teacher's serenity? How valid do you think Siddhartha's argument is?

AWAKENING

Siddhartha walks on, having lost his friend Govinda but with a greater awareness of himself. He is no longer a youth, but a man. He has left behind the greatest of all teachers, Gotama Buddha, and so he has given up all teachers. He has tried in every way to lose or escape or conquer the Self. Now he realizes that the one thing he knows least is himself.

This realization is an awakening to a new life.

He sees for the first time the beauty of the natural world, which his Brahmin teachers taught him to ignore because it was Maya, illusion. Now he sees that if he wishes to know the meaning of the world—and of himself—he must learn the meaning of these shapes and colors in the world of nature.

Then a chilling realization comes over him. He is no longer a Brahmin or a Samana—or a member of any community. He had thought to go home again, but now he knows that all ties, including those to his home and family, are cut. For the first time in his life he is alone. This is the last pang of his awakening. He walks on, no longer looking back.

You can interpret this chapter as Siddhartha's transition from childhood to adulthood, from dependence on parents and teachers—whether in obedience or rebellion—to the independence of maturity. Could you describe this experience in terms of a youth of today making the same transition? Siddhartha may have been seventeen years old when he left home. After spending three years with the Samanas, he is now about twenty. At what age do you think Americans today reach this threshold of independence? Does everyone reach it?

PART TWO
KAMALA

Siddhartha continues his journey through a world of natural beauty that had always existed but of which he was never before aware. He now sees sunrise and sunset, the stars and moon in the night sky, animals mating, birds and insects flying, rivers flowing. He considers the thinking self and the self of the senses and decides that both are essential. This passage is a prose poem of considerable beauty, expressing not only the loveliness of the natural world but Siddhartha's joy of discovery and his delight in wonders that were hidden until now behind a veil of scorn as Maya, illusion.

NOTE: The joy in the natural world and the unaffected poetic language here recall two facts about Hesse: that his early work won him the reputation of a nature novelist, and that he was regarded in Germany as that country's leading poet of the twentieth century. The translation has been credited with doing justice to his poetic style. Notice the unbroken line from the end of the last chapter through the beginning of this one, continuing Siddhartha's journey into this second phase of his quest.

Hesse suffered an eighteen-month writing block after the eighth chapter. Hesse scholars have offered varying explanations of his difficulty in proceeding with the part of the book that resolves Siddhartha's quest. One is that he had not sufficiently clarified his concepts of India. The other is that he had not resolved his own religious philosophy. When you come to the final chapter you will be able to judge how Hesse overcame his difficulties and what religious philosophy he finally developed.

Siddhartha comes to the river and spends the

night in the ferryman's hut. In a dream he embraces Govinda, who in his arms is transformed into a woman. Siddhartha drinks from the woman's breast. The psychoanalytic interpretation here returns to the idea of Govinda as another side of Siddhartha, in this dream the suppressed female side of the male personality. A further, not nec-. essarily contradictory, interpretation is that Siddhartha, already awakened to the sensory world of nature, is now becoming aware of his own sensuality. You may find this convincing, since his next adventure is his discovery of sex.

Siddhartha parts from the ferryman, who tells him he will return—that the river teaches that everything comes back.

NOTE: Rivers have long been a symbol of change. The Greek philosopher Heraclitus (about 535 to 475 B.C.) said that one could not step into the same river twice, that no experiences in life are ever the same. Here the river is seen as a symbol of return, or sameness: everything comes back, the ferryman says, in a cycle of recurrence. How are change and recurrence reconciled in Siddhartha's quest?

Passing through a village, Siddhartha is momentarily drawn to a seductive young woman, but he goes on. Outside the city, in a procession of servants and bearers he sees Kamala, a beautiful courtesan in a sedan chair. Shaved and bathed, but still a half-naked Samana, he gains admittance to her presence. She gives him a kiss for a poem he has written in her honor, and she agrees to teach him the arts of love if he will come back properly dressed and with money and gifts.

Siddhartha is amazed that everything is so easy compared with the hard Samana life. All he must do is acquire clothes and money! The next day even this becomes easy—for Kamala has spoken to Kamaswami, the town's richest merchant, and the man expects Siddhartha. She tells Siddhartha he is lucky, that all doors open to him. It is not luck, says Siddhartha. With the Samanas he learned to let nothing enter his mind except his goal. So, like a stone dropping through water, he is drawn to his goal. Fools call this magic or the work of demons, but there are no demons and everyone can perform magic: "Everyone can reach his goal, if he can think, wait, and fast."

Kamala suggests that it may also be because Siddhartha is handsome and pleases women. You can add other traits that contribute to his good fortune: He has the grace and self-confidence of his princely birth and, most practically, he can read and write. As it turns out, his literacy is what wins him his job with Kamaswami. His other talents later win him success in business.

Still, Siddhartha has some useful advice here for young people everywhere. His single-mindedness, a refusal to be distracted from the pursuit of a desired goal, is a discipline anyone can learn. His self-confidence, which at some moments has come close to arrogance, may be more difficult to acquire, but it is often necessary to put on a show of having it. Still more difficult is his patience: "I can think, I can fast, I can wait." In what ways can these abilities help young people achieve their goals?

What may be especially wholesome in Siddhartha's prescription for success is his dismissal of luck, magic, and demons. Have you known individuals who persistently ascribe their failures to bad luck? Fate is against them, people are out to get them, or they just haven't got what it takes—that they are too nice, too refined, too something or other—to get ahead in this dog-eat-dog world. On the basis of Siddhartha's principle, can you explain what may in fact be wrong with these individuals?

AMONGST THE PEOPLE

Siddhartha's job interview with Kamaswami turns out to be a question-and-answer exchange rather like the posing of riddles and their solutions. For example, when the merchant says that as a Samana and a beggar Siddhartha has lived on the possessions of others, Siddhartha replies that a merchant does the same. Asked what good fasting is, Siddhartha answers that it is useful when a man has nothing to eat.

Notice that in all his conversations at this stage of his life, whether with the Buddha, Kamala, or Kamaswami, Siddhartha is like a bright, quick-witted student, very sure of himself and always ready with an answer. These dialogues are entertaining, but remember that the Buddha warned Siddhartha not to be too clever. What do you think is still missing in Siddhartha's character, apart from the fact that he treats all this as a game?

NOTE: A commentator points out that the title of this chapter in the original is "Amongst the Child-

People," and that the translator has left out the modifier *child*. Siddhartha uses the term later in the novel, but in this chapter he describes the people in the city as childish, concerned with trivial things.

Siddhartha is soon doing business for Kamaswami. When the merchant rebukes him for staying too long in a village where he failed to buy a harvest, Siddhartha acknowledges that he travels for pleasure, makes friends, learns much, and does no harm. Siddhartha treats everyone—his employer or a beggar—as an equal. He has no anxieties, no driving fears or ambitions. This life is still a game to him.

He visits Kamala daily. She teaches him the arts of love, and she thinks she will have a child by him someday. She tells him he is incapable of love, and he says the same is true of her. This is a provocative observation. Why can't Siddhartha and Kamala love? What is missing in their characters? If they don't love each other, what is the nature of their relationship?

SAMSARA

Samsara, in Hindu philosophy, means the life of the world endlessly repeating itself. Siddhartha is living this life. He is rich, with servants, a town house, and a garden by the river. People like him, but only Kamala is close to him. He has not entirely forgotten the Brahmin and Samana disciplines but he has learned the pleasures of the senses.

He enjoys fine clothes, delicate foods, scented baths, watching dancers, and gambling for high stakes.

At first Siddhartha felt superior to the ordinary people who enjoyed these things. Now he is like them, but he also envies them. They feel that their lives are important. They feel joy and sorrow. They have the pain but also the happiness of love—for their children, their goals, themselves. He formerly scorned riches, but now riches have trapped him. He is suffering the discontent and idleness of the rich. To overcome his boredom he seeks the diversions of wine, dancers, and reckless gambling.

He recalls his meeting with the Buddha for Kamala, who can't hear enough about the holy man. Kamala also seems weary of a life with no joyous goal. Siddhartha sees in her face the fine lines of approaching age. He is now forty years old.

That night, after giving a party at which he mocks his guests and drinks too much wine, he has a dream. In it he finds Kamala's little songbird dead in its cage. He takes the tiny body and throws it away, and suddenly feels he has thrown away all that was good and valuable in himself.

He sits all that day under a mango tree in his pleasure garden, recalling the ways of life he has known, remembering the inner voice that led him on. It is a long time since he has heard that voice. He has spent these years sharing the life of the child-people—but without their aims, without their joys and sorrows. Kamala alone is dear to him, but do he and Kamala still need each other? Aren't they, too, playing the game of Samsara, a game that might be enjoyed once or ten times but not endlessly?

That night Siddhartha walks out of his garden, leaving everything behind. Kamaswami searches for him, fearing he has been taken by bandits. Kamala is not surprised at his disappearance. She expected it, especially after their last meeting. Grieving at the loss, she lets her little songbird go free. From then on she closes her house to visitors. Soon after, she finds that she is pregnant with Siddhartha's child.

In his long day and night of self-examination, Siddhartha for the first time acknowledges that ordinary people have things in life that he misses, things of value. What are these things that he envies? Are they of value? What do you think are his causes for despair?

BY THE RIVER

Siddhartha has wandered far from the city, back to the river that he crossed from the other side long ago. He is weak with hunger and fatigue, deep in disgust with himself, longing for death. He is leaning toward the river, about to throw himself in, when a word comes to him: Om. It is the word of meditation with which Brahmin prayers begin and end, the sacred word meaning "Perfection." He is horrified to realize that he was about to commit the ultimate crime, the destruction of divine life. He sinks to the ground amid the roots of a coconut tree and falls deeply, dreamlessly asleep.

He awakens refreshed, a new man, the sickening old life far behind as though it had been a previous incarnation. A monk is sitting nearby, watching over him. He recognizes Govinda, but his friend doesn't recognize him until Siddhartha calls him by name. He tells Govinda that he is a pilgrim. Govinda leaves, to continue his endless wandering as a monk.

Siddhartha is full of love for everything he sees. He is beginning life again, like a child. He has rid himself of his self-hate and self-disgust. Each of his previous lives was necessary in order for him to find his own way. Now the Brahmin priest, the Samana, and the man of pleasure and property have all died within him. Siddhartha himself must one day grow old and die, but today he is young, a new Siddhartha, and he is happy.

This is Siddhartha's second awakening. His first came when he rejected all teaching and discovered the beauty of nature and the need to know himself. That was when he crossed the river the first time. Now he will cross back again.

NOTE: These pages illustrate how Hesse deals with the passage of time in this novel. Although the story moves chronologically, time itself is elastic. Twenty years went by in a few pages, during which Siddhartha changed from a youth just entering manhood to a man in his middle years, his hair already graying. Then, in a night, a day, and another night, the story followed him hour by hour, step by step, through another transformation—but this time from despair and near-suicide to new life and joy. What other passages in the novel contract and expand time?

THE FERRYMAN

Siddhartha has decided that he will not leave the river. It is beautiful and it can teach him. The river is now changing its function in the novel. When Siddhartha crossed it the first time, it was a symbolic as well as a physical boundary, a crossing from the spiritual to the sensual and materialistic experiences in his life. Now it is becoming a source of new wisdom—in effect, a character in the story. It begins to speak to Siddhartha. Is it the river that is speaking, or is it Siddhartha's growing inner awareness? From here on, watch for the succession of truths that he seems to hear the river telling him, eternal truths that are illustrated in the river. One of these he has already learned—that the river is constantly changing and yet always the same. What other truths does he learn, and how does the river illustrate them?

NOTE: Folk and fairy tales were an important aspect of the German Romantic period and of Hesse's educational background. In these tales, inanimate, natural objects such as trees and rocks often speak to the hero. Here the river speaks to Siddhartha. Can you find other analogies to fairy tales in the novel?

The ferryman remembers Siddhartha and tells him his own name is Vasudeva. Siddhartha is moved to confide in Vasudeva, telling him of his childhood, his experiences, his despair and his awakening to new life and love of the river. Vasudeva invites him to stay and share the ferryman's life.

Siddhartha learns to care for the boat. He gathers wood and fruit, works in the rice field, weaves baskets. He learns from the river that time does not pass, that past and future exist together with the present. He hears the voices of all living creatures in the river's voice.

He and Vasudeva come to share their thoughts without speaking. The rumor spreads that two wise or holy men—or magicians—live at the ferry, but travelers who are merely curious find only what they see as two friendly, stupid old men. Years pass.

Followers of the Buddha, hurrying to the side of the dying leader, come to be ferried across the river. Kamala goes on the same pilgrimage with her son, little Siddhartha. She is bitten by a poisonous snake, and Siddhartha cares for her. She dies, leaving the eleven-year-old boy with his father.

The meeting of the two lovers of long ago is tender and moving, but also revealing. Both have reached a new level in their lives. Kamala came this way on a pilgrimage to the Buddha, hoping to find peace in the holy man's presence. She finds it in the presence of Siddhartha, who by now has also found peace.

What do you think is meant by peace? Siddhartha has sought a goal that has been called wisdom, understanding, or losing the self in the universal being. The novel has mentioned bliss, and occasionally salvation, which in Indian religion means being saved from the repetitious life cycle (not from hell and eternal punishment as in Christian belief).

The explanation of peace may come in the passage where Siddhartha reaffirms what the river has told him: that past and future coexist with the present, that every moment is eternal, and that all life is one. The peace that Kamala—and Siddhartha—experience may be an acceptance of the loss of one's individuality in the unity of life.

NOTE: Unity is a basic principle of both Hinduism and Buddhism. Some Hindu sects are so aware of the unity of all life, as well as of its divinity, that they take steps to avoid killing even the tiniest insect. How does this belief in the unity of life compare—as bringing peace of mind—with the Christian and Moslem beliefs in a heavenly life after death for those who earn it?

THE SON

For the first time, Siddhartha is experiencing love, both its joy and its pain, for his son. The boy is accustomed to living in wealth and luxury and having all his wishes granted. He is sulky and defiant toward this old father—a stranger to him—and this father's drastically simple life and menial tasks. Siddhartha hopes to win the boy's affection by kindness and patience. Vasudeva warns him that it will not work, that he must let the boy go his own way.

A day comes when Siddhartha asks the boy to perform a small chore, and the boy turns on him in rage. Soon afterward, little Siddhartha runs away.

Vasudeva has given Siddhartha good parental advice. Little Siddhartha did give up a life of luxury—but not by choice, only because he was obliged to go with his mother. Now he must live with old men who have nothing that the boy values. Siddhartha's love and patience can't win the boy, but can only make him ashamed of his resentment and therefore more resentful. Now Vasudeva advises Siddhartha not to follow the boy. But Siddhartha, made unwise by his love, sets out after his son.

He goes as far as the gate to what had been Kamala's grove. There he stops, reviewing his years spent here until disgust with the life of pleasure had overtaken him. He realizes that he can't force himself on his son. He crouches in the dust, waiting for the pain of loss to subside. Vasudeva finds him and they return together to the ferry.

Little Siddhartha's rebellion against his father recalls Siddhartha's rebellion against his own father. Is this a case merely of a generation gap, or do you see something more in these two situations? What are the similarities and the differences in the two father-son conflicts? A further question arises: Do you find any hints that little Siddhartha will eventually turn from the materialistic life and become a seeker of wisdom like his father?

OM

Siddhartha still feels the pain of his loss. He envies travelers with children whom he ferries across the river. Even criminals have children whom they love and who love them—why not he? He no longer feels superior to ordinary people. Their concerns, however trivial, now win his sympathy, and their vitality and ability to endure suffering win his admiration and love. Sages are different from ordinary people only in their grasp of the unity of all life.

One day, with the wound of his loss especially painful, Siddhartha rows across the river, intending to search again for his son. He hears the river laughing at him. Looking down, he sees his father's face reflected in his own. He is reminded that he left his father as his son has left him. It is a comedy of repetition, and the river is laughing at it. Siddhartha rows back to the hut and confides his pain to Vasudeva. As he does so, he feels his pain being washed away.

Listening to and looking into the river, Siddhartha sees his father, his son, and himself, each alone and lonely. He sees Kamala, Govinda, all yearning, all flowing away in the river. He hears all the voices of humanity blending together into the word *Om* that signifies perfection. When Siddhartha looks again into Vasudeva's face, his own face reflects the same serenity. He is no longer fighting against his destiny and struggling with conflicting desires. He is now full of sympathy and compassion for all creatures. He has surrendered himself to the stream of life and the unity of all things.

NOTE: The phrase "harmony with the stream of events" is used here as a synonym for salvation. The achievement of harmony, whether with life, nature, or the universe, has been the goal of many religions, including both Confucianism and Taoism in China. A Chinese legend tells of an emperor who periodically sent inspectors around the realm to tune all the instruments, in order to keep the empire in harmony. In his last novel, *The Glass Bead Game*, Hesse quotes a Chinese sage as saying that the condition of a nation is revealed by its music. How would you describe Siddhartha's experience of harmony?

Vasudeva now shines with a godlike radiance. He has waited for Siddhartha to arrive at this wisdom. He says farewell and disappears into the woods.

At this culmination of Siddhartha's lifelong quest, how do you think he has in fact won this ultimate wisdom? This chapter traces the stages he has passed through on the road to serenity. But what do these stages represent? What is the meaning of salvation in this context?

GOVINDA

In this last chapter the story focuses on Govinda. Through all these years as a Buddhist monk, Govinda has followed strictly the Buddha's rules, yet he is still restless and seeking. He has heard of an old ferryman who is thought to be a sage, and he now aims his wandering course toward the river.

He asks the old ferryman what doctrine or belief he follows. Again, as when he had watched over Siddhartha sleeping some twenty years before, Govinda does not recognize his boyhood friend. Siddhartha at last reveals his identity.

Siddhartha answers Govinda's question at length. He has no doctrine or teaching. He mistrusts words and even the thoughts that they express. He mistrusts any statement of a so-called truth, because it can express only half of the whole, while the whole embraces its opposite. The saint exists within the sinner. If a stone and a tree are illusion, then Siddhartha is also illusion. He and they are of the same nature, and so he loves them.

When Siddhartha speaks of love, Govinda objects. The Buddha forbade his followers to bind themselves with earthly love. But Siddhartha holds

that Gotama Buddha did indeed know love, that
he loved humanity enough to devote his entire life
to teaching and helping people. The Buddha's
words are less important than his deeds, says Siddhartha.

Govinda is ready to leave. He finds Siddhartha's
ideas strange, even crazy, compared with the
straightforward teachings of the Buddha. But
everything about Siddhartha seems holy—as holy
as the Buddha had been in his lifetime. He asks
Siddhartha to tell him something he can understand, something that will help him on his way,
which is often hard and dark.

Instead of giving Govinda more words, Siddhartha asks Govinda to kiss him on the forehead.
Puzzled, Govinda obeys. Then Govinda has the
strange experience of seeing all kinds of human
beings in all conditions and relationships pass before his eyes, seemingly behind the transparent
film of Siddhartha's serene, smiling face. Deeply
moved and in tears, Govinda recognizes that Siddhartha's smile has reminded him of everything
that he has ever loved and valued in his life.

Here the novel ends, after setting out in this last
chapter a wealth of ideas to consider. As Govinda
says, some of what Siddhartha tells him seems
crazy. It is not orderly and logical like the Buddha's teaching—in other words, it is not a product
of the intellect, but of feeling. Govinda has faith-
fully followed the Buddha's teaching since his
youth, and as an old man he is still suffering, still
seeking. But Siddhartha has found what he sought.
What has he found?

First, notice what Siddhartha has rejected. He
has rejected words, thinking, the formulation of

"truths," because none of these expresses the whole of what is real. In this he has rejected dogma.

He accepts the deeds, the life, the look and gesture of a person—what we might call the body language—as meaningful, rather than what the person says. Does this interpretation make sense to you? How do you judge the feelings, perhaps also the character, of a person? Do you take a person's meaning only from what he or she says?

Siddhartha accepts as real the physical world and the world of feelings and emotions, rather than the world of intellect and theory. Knowledge can be taught, he says, but not wisdom.

He rejects any superiority of one individual over others. All are worthy of admiration, respect, and love.

Love of the world and of people, says Siddhartha, is the most important of all. The peace of understanding comes from accepting the realization that one is not separate or superior or different, but part of the world of people and of life.

NOTE: Love   None of the Eastern religions teaches love. Christianity emphasizes love—man's love of God, God's love for his creatures, and the love of people for each other. Siddhartha tries to reconcile love with Buddhism by seeing it enacted in the Buddha's life, although forbidden in his teaching. Does this convince you? Can you make a case for or against Siddhartha's claim? Maybe Buddhism and Christianity describe different kinds of love. Hesse acknowledged that his eighteen-month block before writing the last part of *Siddhartha* vanished when he decided that Siddhartha would reach his goal by way of love. He made this clear in a 1930 essay, in which he wrote: "My *Siddhartha* glorifies love, and not some form of intellectual awareness. This, together with the book's rejection of dogma and central concern with the experience of unity, could be taken as a return to Christianity. . . ."

What do you make of these conclusions? The novel tells you that they have brought peace and even saintliness to Siddhartha. Perhaps they have brought peace to Govinda as well in this last encounter with his boyhood friend.

Would you agree with Siddhartha and reject all formulas and logical rules for living a life of spiritual satisfaction? Would you trust feeling over thinking, and if so, how far would you rely on feeling, and in what kinds of situations? Siddhartha distinguishes between knowledge and wisdom. Granting that knowledge is gained from teaching and books, what is the source of wisdom?

A STEP BEYOND

Test and Answers

TEST

1. Siddhartha leaves his father's house be-   _____
   cause he
   A. was told to do so in a dream
   B. wants to see the world
   C. wants to join the Samanas

2. The Samanas are   _____
   A. wandering ascetics
   B. teachers of the martial arts
   C. professional musicians

3. Kamala tells Siddhartha to come back when   _____
   he
   A. is hungry   B. has gifts for her
   C. needs a place to stay

4. Govinda parts with Siddhartha in order to   _____
   A. become a Buddhist monk
   B. become a ferryman
   C. go on a pilgrimage

5. Kamaswami hires Siddhartha because he   _____
   can
   A. preach
   B. make a good appearance
   C. read and write

6. Siddhartha does not join the Buddha's fol-   _____
   lowers because he

A. disagrees with the Buddha's teaching
B. wants no teacher
C. thinks the Buddha is a fraud

7. Siddhartha leaves the city because he   _____
   A. has gambled away his wealth
   B. was influenced by an oracle
   C. is sickened by his way of life

8. Little Siddhartha is ashamed because of his   _____
   father's
   A. poverty   B. patience and love
   C. menial job as a ferryman

9. Vasudeva advises the troubled Siddhartha   _____
   to
   A. listen to the river
   B. think good thoughts
   C. rid his soul of evil

10. Kamala, dying, finds peace in   _____
    A. the Buddha's teachings
    B. confessing her sins
    C. Siddhartha's presence

11. Siddhartha learns that love is the most important
    thing in the world. How is love related to the East-
    ern religions? To Christianity?

12. The India of *Siddhartha* has been compared to a fairy
    tale landscape. Describe the setting in terms of the
    classic fairy tale.

13. Discuss the role of the river in *Siddhartha*.

14. Discuss *Siddhartha* as an allegory.

ANSWERS

1. C	2. A	3. B	4. A	5. C	6. B
7. C	8. B	9. A	10. C		

11. Love is not an element in Hinduism, and Buddhism teaches that love and ties of affection and desire are the cause of suffering in life and must be abandoned in order to end suffering and achieve Nirvana. Of the major religions, only Christianity emphasizes love—the love of God, God's love of His people, and love between mankind. Siddhartha's discovery of love is a Christian element in an Indian hero's quest for wisdom. Siddhartha reconciles love with Buddhism by deciding that the Buddha devoted his life to teaching and helping people because he loved them.

12. The setting of *Siddhartha* is an imaginary India modeled on a fairy tale landscape. Its classic elements are the palace of the prince's father, the dangerous forest, the grove of the magician, then the pleasure garden of the siren and the city of wealth and worldly diversions. Symbolically, these can be interpreted further. The palace, the house of the hero's father, represents the established forms and traditions against which the hero rebels. The forest is the scene of Samana ordeals that the hero must overcome. The magician, or sage, in the grove is the Buddha pointing out a different—possibly false—path. Kamala, the siren in the garden, and the city world of business and pleasure are the sensual and materialistic temptations that the hero must undergo as part of his quest for wisdom. Hermann Hesse was familiar with the classic fairy tales assembled by the brothers Grimm and others of the German Romantic Era, and Hesse wrote a number of fairy tales of his own.

13. The river first occurs in the novel as a physical and symbolic boundary between the spiritual world of Hindu ritual, Samana asceticism, and Buddhist teaching, on one side, and the arts of love and the wealth and pleasures of the city on the other. It is incidentally a dividing line between Siddhartha's youth and young manhood, and on his return it again divides his middle years from his old age. When he comes to share Vasudeva's life as a ferryman, the river takes on a new role: it becomes Siddhartha's teacher. He learns to listen to the river and to take the steps toward wisdom that he hears in its voice and sees in the visions it inspires. The river teaches by example. Its waters are constantly new and yet it remains the same, an illustration of how the opposites, change and permanence, can both be true. It flows steadily from past to future and yet it is always present, an example of the illusory nature of time. When Siddhartha hears voices and sees images in the river, he is hearing and seeing reflections of his own inner processes of thought and feeling as he strives toward the peace of understanding.

14. *Siddhartha* has been compared to *The Pilgrim's Progress*, a seventeenth-century religious allegory telling the story of a man named Christian's journey through life, through perilous places such as the Slough of Despond and the Valley of the Shadow of Death. *Siddhartha* is the story of a similar journey. The characters' Indian names have cleary allegorical meanings. Kamala, the name of the beautiful courtesan, means sensual love. Kamaswami, Siddhartha's rich merchant employer, translates as master of the material world. The wise ferryman Vasudeva is "he in whom all things abide and who abides in all things." Siddhartha's friend and follower, Govinda, is a "keeper of cows," and as cows are sacred in Hinduism, this suggests a religious person, although one of humble rank. Siddhartha himself is "he who is on the right road" or, alternatively, "he who attains his goal." The forest where Siddhartha practices asceticism with the Samanas, the grove where he meets the Buddha and rejects Buddhism, and the city where he experiences worldly success and sensual pleasures are comparable to the dangerous or seductive places through which Christian in *The Pilgrim's Progress* passes. In contrast to Christian's goal of salvation and reaching heaven, however, is Siddhartha's goal of understanding and peace. He achieves this at the river, which flows between the spiritual and material worlds and embraces the experience of both.

Glossary
FOR *SIDDHARTHA*

Agni Hindu god of fire.

Aryan (Sanskrit for noble) Asian people believed to have brought Hinduism into India about 1500 B.C.

Asceticism Self-denial of all sensory pleasures, including food except for the minimum needed for survival. A way of life, usually for religious reasons.

Asoka, 264?–226? B.C., and his son, Mahendra Enlightened Indian monarchs who spread Buddhism in India and Sri Lanka.

Atharva-Veda *See* VEDAS.

Atman In Hindu belief, the Universal Soul or Self. The essence of the individual self and the universal self.

Bo tree Old World tree under which Buddha experienced Enlightenment.

Brahma In Hindu belief, the Supreme Being.

Brahman, Brahmin Member of the highest, priestly Hindu caste.

Buddha The Enlightened One, founder of Buddhism.

Eightfold Path and Four Noble Truths Teachings of Buddha (see p. 67).

Gotama (Gautama) Family name of the Buddha.

Jetavana Grove in which the Buddha preached.

Kama Hindu god of sensual love.

Karma In Hindu and Buddhist belief, the destiny of the individual determined by deeds in a previous incarnation.

Krishna One of the incarnations (avatars) of the Hindu god Vishnu the Preserver.

Lakshmi Hindu goddess of beauty and luck.

Maya In Hindu belief, the illusory physical world.

Nirvana In Hinduism and Buddhism, a state of blissful nonexistence or release from the sensual world and suffering.

Om Perfection, the word of meditation, which begins and ends Hindu prayers.

Pali Sanskrit dialect of Buddhist scriptures, believed to be Buddha's language.

Prajaparti In Hindu belief, the Creator.

Rig-Veda *See* VEDAS.

Sakya The Buddha's clan. Sakyamuni, "wise man of the Sakyas," is one of the Buddha's names.

Sallow Old World willow.

Salvation religions Late Hindu sects promising release from the cycle of rebirths.

Samanas Sect of ascetic, wandering beggars.

Samsara, Sansara In Hindu and Buddhist belief, the physical world, characterized by repeated cycles of birth (reincarnation).

Sanskrit India's ancient literary language and the language of the Hindu scriptures.

Upanishads Poetic dialogues added to the Vedas as commentaries and philosophic discourses.

Vedas The original Hindu scriptures.

Steppenwolf and Siddhartha

Term Paper Ideas and other Topics for Writing

On *Steppenwolf*

1. *Steppenwolf* is described as the most autobiographical of Hesse's novels. Drawing on Hesse's biography, discuss the similarities and/or differences between Harry Haller and Hesse.

2. *Steppenwolf* has been called a psychoanalytic novel. Discuss Hesse's psychoanalytic influences in terms of the novel's content.

3. Describe the "framework" form of *Steppenwolf* and its literary purpose.

4. Discuss Hermann Hesse's 1942 "Postscript to *Steppenwolf*," which says that it is a novel of healing and hope. Do you agree or disagree?

5. Describe the three first-person narrators of *Steppenwolf*, in terms of point of view and writing style. What does the author accomplish by using three different voices?

6. Choose three of Harry's experiences in the Magic Theater, and analyze their possible meanings.

7. Harry detests the middle class and yet chooses to live in middle-class surroundings. Describe Harry's contradictory attitudes.

8. Describe the various changes in Hermine, Maria, and Pablo as they occur in "reality," at the Masked Ball, and in the Magic Theater.

9. *Steppenwolf* has been compared with Goethe's *Faust*. What are the similarities and differences?

On *Siddhartha*

1. As he pursues his quest, Siddhartha states his goal in different terms at different stages. Discuss the relation between these stages and his goals.

2. Compare *Siddhartha* with the classic Christian allegory, *The Pilgrim's Progress*.

3. Siddhartha leaves his father, and then Siddhartha's son leaves him. Discuss the novel's father-son relationships.

4. Kamala and Siddhartha agree that neither of them is capable of love. What is the quality that they lack, and how does Siddhartha overcome this deficiency?

On *Steppenwolf* and *Siddhartha*

1. Describe Hesse's treatment of time in both novels.

2. Compare Hermine and Kamala, the similarities and differences in their characters, and their relationship with the hero in each novel.

3. Transformations from one sex to the other occur in both novels. Describe these episodes. What is their meaning?

4. Hesse uses different devices for dividing reality from fantasy and spirituality from materialism in the two novels. Explore his methods.

5. Harry Haller hears the laughter of the Immortals, and Siddhartha hears the laughter of the river. What is the meaning of laughter in each novel?

Further Reading

BIOGRAPHIES OF HERMANN HESSE

Freedman, Ralph. *Hermann Hesse: Pilgrim of Crisis*. New York: Pantheon Books, 1978. Filled with interesting insights into Hesse's work.

Mileck, Joseph. *Hermann Hesse: Life and Art*. Berkeley: University of California Press, 1978. The work of a renowned Hesse scholar.

CRITICAL WORKS

Boulby, Mark. *Hermann Hesse: His Mind and Art*. Ithaca, New York: Cornell University Press, 1967. Detailed studies of Hesse's novels.

Casebeer, Edwin F. *Hermann Hesse*. New York: Thomas Y. Crowell, 1972. In the "Writers for the Seventies" series. Studies of *Siddhartha, Steppenwolf, Narcissus and Goldmund*, and *Magister Ludi* (*The Glass Bead Game*).

Fickert, Kurt J. *Hermann Hesse's Quest: The Evolution of the Dichter* (*Poet*) *Figure in His Work*. Fredericton, New Brunswick, Canada: York Press, 1978. A concise academic study.

Field, George W. *Hermann Hesse*. New York: Twayne, 1970. Biography and analysis of the fiction.

Freedman, Ralph. *The Lyrical Novel*. Princeton: Princeton University Press, 1963. Discussions of the novels by a Hesse biographer.

Mileck, Joseph. *Hermann Hesse and His Critics*. Chapel Hill, North Carolina: University of North Carolina Press, 1958.

Otten, Anna, ed. *Hesse Companion*. Albuquerque: University of New Mexico Press, 1977. A biographical study and essays, by Theodore Ziolkowski on *Siddhartha* and Mark Boulby on *Steppenwolf*, among others.

Ziolkowski, Theodore, ed. *Hesse: A Collection of Critical Essays*. Englewood Cliffs, New Jersey: Prentice-Hall, 1973. Essays on Hesse by Thomas Mann, André Gide, and Martin Buber, among others, with a valuable introduction by the editor.

Ziolkowski, Theodore. *The Novels of Hermann Hesse*. Princeton: Princeton University Press, 1965. Analyses of the novels from *Demian* to *The Glass Bead Game*, including *Siddhartha* and *Steppenwolf*.

AUTHOR'S SELECTED OTHER WORKS

Fiction

Peter Camenzind (1904) A youthful novel of a young man's rejection of the world for the life of a nature hermit.

Beneath the Wheel (German *Unterm Rad*, 1906) Fictionalized version of Hesse's schoolboy life, a harsh picture of the educational system.

Gertrud (1910) The first of Hesse's "artist novels," in which two friends, a composer and a singer, love the same woman, also a musician.

Rosshalde (1914) A second "artist novel," this one of a painter struggling with an unhappy marriage.

Knulp (1915) Three tales of a charming homeless rogue.

Demian: The Story of a Youth (1919) Hesse's first novel after his psychoanalysis, signed by the pen name Emil

Sinclair. Story of growing up in a southern German town like Hesse's boyhood home.

Narcissus and Goldmund (German *Narziss und Goldmund*, 1930) An "artist novel," the story of a sculptor in a medieval monastery.

The Journey to the East (German *Die Morgenlandfahrt*, 1932) A short novel of a fantastic journey through time as well as space, with historical (Plato, Tolstoy) and fictional (Don Quixote, Tristram Shandy) companions, among them Hesse's own Siddhartha, Vasudeva, and Pablo disguised as Mozart.

The Glass Bead Game, also translated as *Magister Ludi* (German *Das Glasperlenspiel*, 1943) Hesse's last novel takes place in a utopian enclave of artists and intellectuals, in a mythical land of the future called Castalia.

Other

Autobiographical Writings Edited and with an introduction by Theodore Ziolkowski. Translated by Denver Lindley. New York: Farrar, Straus, and Giroux, 1972.

My Belief: Essays on Life and Art Edited and with an introduction by Theodore Ziolkowski. Translated by Denver Lindley and Ralph Manheim. New York: Farrar, Straus, and Giroux, 1974.

Poems Selected and translated by James Wright. New York: Farrar, Straus, and Giroux, 1970.

The Critics

On *Steppenwolf*

Thomas Mann remarked of *The Steppenwolf* that it was a book not inferior in its experimental boldness to *Ulysses* or *Les Fauxmonnayeurs* [*The Counterfeiters*]. Certainly it depends for its effect upon an artistic principle very different from that which informs *Siddhartha*. The extremely conscious structure, the massive intrusions of reflective commentary through the bourgeois narrator, through the tractate [treatise], through Harry's obsessional process of self-diagnosis, the discourses of Hermine, Pablo, and the chess player, and a speculation about music as a German heritage in which Harry's reflection all but cracks the taut framework of the novel—all this shows the bent of the book. . . . *The Steppenwolf*, one must sum up, is an act of faith imposing form on chaos, time on space, and music on life . . . by the apotheosis of irony.

> —Mark Boulby in *Hermann Hesse:*
> *His Mind and Art*, 1967

In much of his post-war fiction prior to [*Steppenwolf*], Hesse's rejection of contemporary civilization had been negative. His heroes were made to withdraw from its values either into the Orient or into an oddly anachronistic world compounded of the Middle Ages and the romantic nineteenth century prior to the industrial revolution. But *Der Steppenwolf* uses the theme of the artist's alienation directly by dwelling on the hero's encounters within the hostile world itself. It is Hesse's only major work to deal exclusively with a twentieth-century urban environment and to exploit its major symbols: jazz music, asphalt streets, electric lights, bars, motion pictures, and night clubs. . . . *Der Steppenwolf* views urban life as symbolic of modern man's cultural and psychological disintegration. Signifying an important, if passing, phase in Hesse's work, it replaces withdrawal with revolt. It expresses the artist's rebellion against a humorless culture.

> —Ralph Freedman, *The Lyrical*
> *Novel*, 1963

On *Siddhartha*

It is no surprise that Hesse undertook to write a novel about India. By the same token it would be naive to read the book as an embodiment or exegesis of Indian philosophy. Hesse found this book difficult to compose because he was engaged in coming to terms with India as he wrote. *Demian* was poured forth within the period of a few months in 1917; *Siddhartha: An Indic Poem* required almost four years of effort although it is shorter than *Demian* by one quarter. . . . It was not until 1922, after a complete revision of his views of India, that Hesse was finally able to finish the last third of his novel. . . . The highest lesson of the novel is a direct contradiction of Buddha's theory of the Eightfold Path, to which . . . Hesse objected in his diary of 1920; it is the whole meaning of the book that Siddhartha can attain Buddha's goal without following his path. . . . Just as Siddhartha learns of the totality and simultaneity of all being—man and nature alike—so too the development of the soul is expressed in geographical terms and, in turn, the landscape is reflected in the human face. The book achieves a unity of style, structure, and meaning that Hesse never again attained with such perfection after *Siddhartha*. . . . In *Siddhartha* he reached an extreme of symbolic lyricism; his next major work, *The Steppenwolf*, comes closer to realism in its characterization, dialogue, and plot than anything else Hesse has written.

—Theodore Ziolkowski, *The Novels of Hermann Hesse*, 1965

Steppenwolf and Psychoanalysis

The Steppenwolf concept . . . was immediately intertwined with Hesse's own feelings about himself as a man, but basically it remained a construct for a book. It was the key by which his life gained entry into his art. Hermann Hesse, who felt isolated and depressed, was the *person*. His Steppenwolf-protagonist, Harry Haller, who played with these feelings in art, became the *persona*. In the curious metamorphosis that transforms a life into a novel, the *pathology* of the first became the *imagination* of the second. The two are not identical. *Steppenwolf* is indeed the record of a crisis, but it is also more than that.

It is a crisis transformed. The personal origins of the novel . . . may be found in Hesse's inability to re-establish a coherent personal life after his break with the past in 1919 . . . It was a time of physical and psychic pain, accompanied by a sense of spiritual emptiness, a conviction . . . that he had once again lost his creative powers. This psychic matter, which seems to have molded him as a person, Hesse clearly experienced in psychoanalytic terms, despite his disclaimer. . . . Harry Haller's world is largely *within*—the Magic Theater and its strange protago-nists are part of his psyche—and the novel con-stantly tests the internal against an external real-ity. . . . Haller's pilgrimage resembles that of psychoanalytic education. He seeks his ascent, and experiences his failure, among *mirrors* . . . which reflect various aspects of himself.

—Ralph Freedman, *"Person and Persona, the Magic Mirrors of Steppenwolf,"* in *Hesse: A Collection of Critical Essays,* 1973

Hesse in the 1960s

The Hesse phenomenon has also brought the lit-erary critics to the barricades. Stephen Koch, writ-ing in the *New Republic* (July 13, 1968), points out that the young generation's "capacity for cultural co-option scares the hell out of a lot of people, my-self sometimes included." While conceding that "the final third of *Steppenwolf* is one of the great moments of modern literature," Koch asserts that "Hesse's thought is irretrievably adolescent, so that in his chosen role of artist of ideas, he is inevitably sec-ond-rate. . . ." Koch is annoyed not so much at Hesse himself, who "despite his faults . . . is a graceful and generally unpretentious artist." He is dis-mayed, rather, by what he regards as Hesse's per-nicious influence on the young, who had adopted him as their spiritual leader. George Steiner, re-porting on the Hesse vogue in *The New Yorker* (Jan-uary 18, 1969), concedes that there are certain "memorable passages" in *Steppenwolf* and singles out *The Glass Bead Game* . . . as "the masterful exception" in Hesse's work. But like Koch, Steiner is not really talking about Hesse at all. What bothers Steiner, straight from a visit to a hippie commune in Haight-Ashbury, is the fact that "The young have read little and compared less. Stringency is not their forte. Like prayer bells and beads, like pot and love-ins, Hesse seems to offer ecstasy and transcendence on the easy-payment plan." . . . It should be readily evident that Hesse criticism cannot be dissociated wholly from the Hesse cult among the young, for to a conspicuous extent much recent criticism is a direct response to that cult—to a sociological situation, not a literary one. . . .

> —Theodore Ziolkowski,
> Introduction, *Hesse: A Collection of Critical Essays*, 1973

A Minor Writer

Hesse is, by any severe artistic or intellectual standards, a minor writer, although not an uninteresting one if regarded with proper skepticism and a sufficient knowledge of his context. For all his high-mindedness and humaneness, his consciousness unwittingly reflects ideological positions that have had catastrophic consequences. . . . There is always a kind of shrinkage in Hesse from the consequences of the doctrines he is experimenting with; they are blunted by crossing them with incompatible doctrines, or they are made ultimately inconsequential by being placed in a play of the imagination that is intransitive because it is hermetically sealed from the detested world outside. His effect is to sugar-coat the dynamite of the German irrational tradition, and there is plenty of evidence that when that tradition is turned into pablum, those who overindulge in it are likely to wake up with a cosmic stomach ache.

> —Jeffrey L. Sammons, "Hermann Hesse and the Over-Thirty Germanist" in *Hesse: A Collection of Critical Essays*, 1973